Automatic Marketing

How to build a robotic, hands-free selling machine

Benjamin Hart

Profit Books

1.800.599.5150

McLean, Virginia

Email: lovesdirectmail@aol.com

For information and other requests please write:

Profit Books
1390 Chain Bridge Road, 22
McLean, Virginia 22101

Or call: **800.599.5150**
You may also email orders and requests to:
lovesdirectmail@aol.com

Printed in the United States of America by:

Signature Book Printing, Inc.
www.sbpbooks.com

Contents

1. Let's first understand the true definition of marketing   5

2. The four essential elements of a successful
    marketing campaign   9

3. The most important question you must answer
    before you launch your marketing campaign   13

4. If you can't precisely measure your marketing,
    it's <u>not</u> marketing. It's public relations   15

5. The five stages of your marketing strategy   17

6. What we can learn from the Grateful Dead   23

7. Avoid the price-cutting trap   27

8. Be a relentless collector of testimonials   35

9. Turn your business into a
    "Referral Generation Factory"   37

10. How to generate leads . . . other than
    with referrals   53

11. Make your marketing robotic, automatic,
    and hands-free   63

12. How to use the Internet to automate
    your marketing   81

13. How to use voice and video to inject
    rocket fuel into your marketing   101

14. The power of electronic seminars   105

Contents

15. Your monthly newsletter is the next best thing to printing money in your basement   111

16. Three essential rules of marketing   115

17. The nine-step formula for writing successful sales letters   119

18. Seventeen reasons people buy . . . plus the #1 reason people buy   129

19. The Offer   137

20. The critical importance of "Positioning"   145

21. How to write a great sales letter   149

22. Letters to business executives   177

23. The science of persuasion   181

24. The most important word in direct marketing   191

25. Narrow is the gate to paradise   193

26. How to find the money in your customer list   197

27. How to rent lists to prospect for new customers   211

28. Summing up   219

Appendix One
Your marketing checklist   223

Appendix Two
Your marketing tool kit   227

Chapter One

Let's first understand
the true definition of marketing

Marketing is not sales.

Sales is an element of marketing. But if your marketing is done right, you should never need to make another sales call. You'll just be taking in orders and shipping product. Or you'll just be accepting the jobs you want to do. No more scrambling for work. No more wondering how the bills for next month will be paid.

Marketing is not really selling at all.

Marketing is the process of putting bait in the water to attract leads, and then putting your leads into a sifting and sorting system that will allow you to identify your most likely customers. You then keep putting yourself and your product in front of your most qualified leads until *they* want to buy. You give your leads great information in the form of news-letters and emails that will keep them interested—not heavy-handed sales pitches, but valuable free information that they look forward to receiving.

This, in summary, is how you transform yourself from being an annoying pest into a welcome guest in your prospect's home. That's marketing, not sales.

Yes, sales are the end result of all your marketing. Certainly you can't make a penny until a sale is made. The sale is everything in business. The sale is the one and only goal of all business. But you are no longer a salesman. You are a marketer. And there's a world of difference.

Good marketers are rich. Salesmen are almost all poor and strug-gling, like Willie Loman in Arthur Miller's *Death of a Salesman*. Not a happy story. You don't want to be Willie Loman. You want to be Bill Gates, Ross Perot, or Donald Trump. These men are marketers. These men don't make sales calls. And neither should you.

Even if you are in a sales position—say, selling cars or selling houses—never think of yourself as a salesman. The great salesmen are really marketers. They aren't pounding the pavement and making cold calls. Marketing is working smart. Selling is working stupid.

Be a marketer, not a salesman. Study marketing. Live and breathe marketing. And your life will be so much more pleasant and lucrative.

Marketing is your strategy. Marketing is your roadmap. Marketing is your system. Marketing is all that goes into laying the groundwork and establishing the preconditions that end in a sale.

And if the marketing is done right, you don't really need a sales force. What you need are customer service people and order takers. What you need is a mechanism, a system, to handle all the business that pours in, seemingly magically, seemingly on its own, almost out of thin air.

Except it's not magic, on its own, or out of thin air.

The customers and clients that will line up at your door and swamp your business are the result of careful planning and execution of your overall marketing strategy.

This little book will show you how to develop a very powerful marketing strategy that will work for any business, whether it's a one-man or one-woman operation . . . or a large corporation.

The true mission of all business

Most companies have a marketing division, a product development division, and a customer service division. Most companies think of these as three separate and distinct functions.

Very often the product development people never talk to the marketing people and the marketing people never talk to the product development people. Meanwhile, the customer service people have almost no stature in the company and are thought of mainly as clerks.

There are also administrative people who do things like accounting and make sure the elevators work and that everyone has a computer and a desk. The administrative people often have little idea of what the company even does, much less any sense of the marketing strategy.

What catastrophic mistakes these are.

Marketing should never be a "division" or a "department" within a company. Instead, the entire company should be about marketing. Everyone in the company should be involved in marketing. A receptionist is not a low-wage worker; he or she is one of your vital marketers.

Your receptionist and those who answer the phones are the voice of your company to your customers and clients.

Your accounting people are not bean counters, but should be integrally involved in making your marketing more efficient and productive. Everyone in every company should understand that their paychecks come from one and only one source: *customers*.

Without customers, without sales, there are no paychecks.

Everyone in every company should be thinking all the time about how to create happy experiences for customers. Everyone in the company should be first and foremost a marketer.

The chairman of the company should think of almost nothing else but marketing. The product development people should think of marketing first when they develop their products. What good is it to develop a great product or provide a great service that no one wants?

All products must be developed with the market for the product at the forefront. "Do our prospects and customers want this thing we're making?" is the question the product development people must always ask.

Meanwhile, the finance people, the accountants, and the lawyers should not ask, "How can we make our lives easier?" Instead they should ask, "How can we make it easier for people to do business with us? Do we really need to require our customers to fill out all these forms when they buy? Do we really need to require our customers to sign long agreements that no one reads? Do we really need these awful disclaimers in tiny print on our order forms?"

The janitor is not a janitor. A janitor is a key marketing person whose job is to make sure the place looks neat and clean—like a company people will want to do business with.

No matter what business you are in, your company should be a marketing company first—because marketing by definition means "creating happy customers and clients."

Making cars, windows, or widgets is not the mission of your business. "Finding and nurturing happy customers" is the true mission of all business. Solving your customer's problem is your mission. Supplying what your customer wants is your mission. Making great and wonderful widgets is just the means to that end.

So now we've dispensed with the need to come up with a mission statement for your company. The mission statement for every business should be: "We are dedicated to creating wonderful experiences for our customers." In other words, we are dedicated to marketing.

Are you starting to see how this mindset is very different from the "selling" mindset?

The goal of your company, your business, is not just to make transactions (sales). The goal of your business should be to build an ongoing relationship with your customers—to turn customers into clients. You want long-term clients, not one-time customers. You want ongoing relationships with loyal clients, not a series of impersonal transactions with customers you don't know and who don't know you. Salesmen pound the pavement and make cold calls to get transactions. Marketers aim for nurturing relationships with their first-time buyers so customers will become loyal clients and repeat buyers for the rest of their lives.

Marketers understand that where there is a relationship, there is no competition.

This book will teach you strategies and methods for finding first-time customers and then how to transform your customers into loyal lifetime clients who would never think of doing business with your competitors. Furthermore, this book will show you how to do this by creating systems and using technologies that will make 80 percent of your marketing and selling automatic, robotic, and hands-free.

But before we talk systems and technologies, let's first go over the marketing basics—basics that have been known now for well over a century. The essential marketing basics never change. Delivery mechanisms change, but not the basic marketing principles.

Chapter Two

The four essential elements of a successful marketing campaign

Your marketing campaign will be successful if it has these four essential elements:

1. You must offer a product or service that people want.

This may seem obvious, and is just another way of saying, "You'll have a very difficult time selling ice to Eskimos or down parkas to people who live in Ecuador."

It's amazing how many business people keep pounding their heads against the wall trying to persuade people to want their wonderful product. Those businesses are not around long.

The greatest marketing plan and salesmen in the world won't succeed in selling products people don't want. This is why your product development people must also be marketers.

So often I've seen brilliant software architects scream, howl, jump up and down, and treat the client like he's an idiot when the client doesn't like the software. "This software is great! This software is brilliant!" screams the software architect. "Why can't they see that?"

The problem is the client doesn't like the software, doesn't need it, doesn't want it, and wasn't looking for it. And there is nothing a marketer can do to change that fact. Much better to find out what the customers want first, and then develop the product tailored precisely and exactly to what they want. This is called "market research."

The product or service you are selling is critical to your marketing. The #1 rule of successful marketing is: *If you offer people what they want, you eliminate the need for salesmanship.*

2. You must have an attention-getting, compelling message that distinguishes you from your competitors.

People are bombarded all day long with messages—TV ads, radio ads, junk mail ads, and Internet ads. You must have a message that stands out. You must have a message that gets the attention of those who would want your product . . . if they knew about it.

3. You must have a way to find those who want what you are offering.

If you have no way to systematically and precisely find those who would want your product or service if they knew about it, your business will have a very tough time surviving. You must match your message to those who will be interested in hearing your message.

You must have a "Message to Market Match."

This is just another way of saying you need a list of qualified prospects or leads, or you need a way of compiling such a list. There are two ways you can find qualified prospects. You can rent lists of people who have bought similar products to the one you are selling. The mailing list business is an enormous industry. So that's one source of names.

The other way is to compile your own one-of-a-kind list. There are many ways to do this, which I will get into later. The point here is that acquiring or compiling a list of qualified prospects or leads is essential to your marketing.

4. You must have a cost-effective delivery system for your message.

Delivery tools at your disposal for getting your message out include: direct mail, email, radio ads, TV ads, newspaper and magazine ads, ads on the Internet, the telephone, the Yellow Pages, classified ads, seminars, webinars, teleconferences, books, special reports, newsletters, business cards, bulletin boards, signs, and even the door-to-door sales calls (which we want to avoid). And there are countless variations within these categories.

You will need to choose the delivery tool that's appropriate for your business model, product, and budget. A hammer is a great tool if you want to drive a nail into a piece of wood, but a very bad tool if you need to saw the wood in half.

This book will show you how to match the tool to the job at hand.

And when I say a "cost-effective" delivery system, I don't mean go out and find the cheapest system. If you spend $100,000 in advertising and bring in $200,000 in profit, that's cost-effective marketing. On the other hand, if you spend $10 and get no response, that's not cost-effective at all.

All that matters is how much you spent on your marketing and how much profit (not gross revenue) came in. In other words, what is your return on each marketing dollar spent?

You must always know precisely the answer to this last question.

If these four elements are present in your marketing campaign, you will be successful.

Chapter Three

The most important question you must answer before you launch your marketing campaign

You **cannot write an effective** sales letter or advertisment until you answer one question.

Once you've answered this question, your letter will almost write itself. This question is: **"What am I really selling?"**

Am I selling cosmetics? Or am I selling the hope of the reader becoming irresistible to men?

Am I selling clothes? Or am I selling a transformed life that will lead to romance and success?

Am a selling a car? Or am I selling excitement, comfort, and an image for the driver?

Am I selling refrigerators? Or am I selling fewer trips to the grocery store because of all the added space, plus dramatically improving the appearance of the kitchen because of the fine cherry wood paneling?

Am I selling vacations? Or am I selling an experience that the reader and her children will remember for the rest of their lives?

Am I selling gym memberships with treadmills and weights? Or am I selling a new body that will make people more attractive to the opposite sex and give them a longer, healthier life?

Am I selling a seminar? Or am I selling a way to give those who enroll an advantage over their peers and competitors that will last a lifetime?

Am I selling admission to Harvard? Or membership in an exclusive club that will lead to a more profitable career and open the doors of opportunity throughout life?

Am I selling a subscription to an interesting magazine? Or access to information the reader can't do without and can't get anywhere else?

Is Starbucks selling coffee? Or is Starbucks selling an experience, a place to hang out, and even a social life?

Are florists selling roses? Or the easiest way for a guy to get back on the good side of his wife or girlfriend?

Is the phone company selling communications equipment? Or a way to stay connected to friends and loved ones?

Is Viagra selling a fix for erectile dysfunction? Or a more exciting, more enjoyable love life?

Understanding exactly what it is you are really selling will improve the results of your marketing exponentially.

Chapter Four

If you can't precisely measure your marketing, it's <u>not</u> marketing. It's public relations

True marketing is trackable. True marketing is measurable to the penny.

To be a true marketer you must know exactly how much it costs you to generate an order. For marketing to be precisely measurable, it must be direct response marketing. It cannot be the image and brand awareness advertising we see from Madison Avenue that the big corporations use.

For example, Nike's ads do not ask us to do anything except memorize its logo. Nike has no idea how many sales each ad is producing because there is no way for anyone to answer a Nike ad. Nike is not asking for an answer. All Nike wants is for us to remember the name of the company and that "swoosh" symbol.

This kind of advertising certainly does work for enormous worldwide corporations such as Nike, Coca-Cola and McDonald's because these companies have billion-dollar advertising budgets. And these companies have global distribution for their products—enormous multi-billion-dollar infrastructures. If you go into a shoe or sports store, Nike products are everywhere. Coca-Cola is everywhere; so is McDonald's. Image advertising works for them.

But you and I don't have a billion-dollar advertising budget.

You and I must be careful with our marketing dollars. You and I don't have enough money or time to build up brand recognition, like Nike or Coke. You and I must be surgical. Our marketing must be launched with laser-like precision. We must aim our marketing precisely at those who are most likely to buy what we are offering. We must know to the penny what it costs to bring in a customer. We must also know with precision the average lifetime value of the customers we bring in. We must have systems in place to track and measure all our marketing.

I don't want to spend a penny on general image building or public relations, because I'll have no idea what I'm getting for my money in terms of actual sales.

Here are a few numbers you will certainly need to track:

> The number of leads it takes to find a customer;

> How much each lead is costing you;

> What sources of advertising are producing the most leads for each dollar spent; and

> What sources and ads are generating the most productive leads.

And you must religiously put all these numbers into a computer database so you can track your progress from month to month.

But here's another benefit of measuring and tracking all your marketing efforts. You will find that anything you measure automatically improves. Whatever you stop measuring automatically decays and gets worse. If you want to see improvement, start measuring what you want improved.

And post the numbers you are tracking in scoreboard fashion prominently at your company. Your employees will pay close attention to these numbers. And they will appreciate knowing exactly what the goals of your company are. Your employees don't want to fly in the fog anymore than you do. They want to do a good job for you. But they can't do a good job if they don't know what success is. Everything will improve when everyone knows what numbers the company (the boss) is tracking.

Chapter Five

The five stages of your marketing strategy

You must think of your marketing strategy as having five distinct phases.

1. Finding qualified leads

You only want to spend money marketing your product to those you know are looking for what you are offering. There's no point in trying to sell a steak dinner to people who aren't hungry and don't especially like steak. Focus on those you know are hungry and who you know love steak.

One way to find out who the steak lovers are is to offer a free steak.

That's what Morton's steak house does. Every so often I receive a coupon in the mail from Morton's offering me a free steak if I bring a guest and order dinner for my guest. That's an attractive offer. Morton's is one of my favorite restaurants anyway. So I always take Morton's up on the offer. This tactic does several good things for Morton's.

First, the offer is only good during the week when Morton's is not likely to be full anyway, so Morton's isn't losing much. Morton's also knows I'll be buying all kinds of things when I go in. I'll be buying a full dinner for my guest. I'll also buy wine, coffee, desert, and my final bill will still be in excess of $100. So Morton's probably is not losing any money on the offer.

Morton's is also finding out who the steak lovers are with this offer. If you don't like steak, you're not going to be impressed with an offer of a free steak.

Second, Morton's is doing something nice for its customers. I have a good feeling about Morton's because of the free steak. And I always have a good experience at Morton's. I would not have gone on that particular night without the free steak offer. By going to Morton's, I am reminded of the good experience I have whenever I go to Morton's. The more going to Morton's becomes a habit for me, the more money Morton's will make from me. Offering something free is great bait to attract qualified leads.

On the Internet, you always see free special reports and free books offered. These are excellent items to offer because special reports and even books are relatively inexpensive to produce and because most people go on the Internet to look for information on subjects, products, or services that interest them; that they want to buy.

Offering a free Buyer's Guide on_____, a free Consumer's Report on_____, a free Special Report on_____, or a free book on_____, is a highly-effective method of attracting leads on the Internet. You can do this with banner ads on sites that are of interest to your target audience or with skillful use of Google AdWords or Yahoo's Overture. With Google AdWords and Overture, you bid on keywords and phrases associated with the ad you are writing. When the keywords and phrases are typed in, your ad pops up, listed in the same order as your keywords bid. If you are the tenth highest bidder for that particular keyword or phrase, that's the order your ad will appear. I'll discuss Google AdWords, Overture, and search engine rankings later in this book. These are all valuable lead generation tools for certain kinds of products and services—the more specialized and niche focused the product is, the better.

You can also offer free special reports, free consumer guides, free books, free samples, and free services with ads in the Yellow Pages, newspapers, classified ads, or via direct mail. All these advertising media will be covered later in this book. The main point here is that offering something of value free is great bait for attracting leads. One reason this is particularly effective on the Internet is that those who find the bait had to be looking specifically for the product or service you are selling. This makes an Internet-generated lead especially qualified.

Once you've hooked your lead, the cultivating, sifting, sorting, and classifying can begin.

2. Cultivating your prospects before the first sale

The way you cultivate your prospect is to continue to give her a lot of valuable free information on the subject that you know she is interested in. Remember, people love to be educated and informed in an honest way about subjects that interest them. They don't like to be sold. When the selling starts, the prospect shuts down.

You are an expert in whatever it is you are selling. Your lead has already shown she's interested in this subject. So keep feeding her unbiased, factual, interesting, and valuable information on this subject. Keep feeding her more of the same bait you hooked her with. Even though intellectually she knows you are in business to sell, she will begin to see you as an honest source of information. She will begin to trust you.

If you are selling wine, send a monthly newsletter on wine and invitations to wine tastings. If you are a pest exterminator, send a monthly newsletter on all the nasty critters that are living in everyone's homes and the latest developments in pest control. If you are a plastic surgeon, send a newsletter on all the things that are being done in plastic surgery.

Your prospect is like a piece of string that you must pull gently up a hill. Never push a string. A customer, like a delicate piece of thread, can only be pulled, gently. The second your prospect feels she is being pushed is the second her defenses go up.

Your prospect has not bought from you yet for the simple reason that she's not ready to buy from you yet. She's interested. She likes the information she's getting from you. Your job is to be the first one she thinks of when she's ready to buy. You want to be at the top of her list.

If she feels she's already received great value from you for free, the chances are 80 percent that she will buy from you and not your competitor when she's ready—but not a minute sooner. If you push, you'll destroy your credibility and the relationship you've been cultivating.

Remember, you always want to be a welcome guest, not an annoying pest.

3. Making the first sale

The sale is the goal of all business. You have not really achieved anything until a sale is made. This is victory.

I'm not going to discuss all the techniques for closing a sale here . . . because if you've done your marketing job right, you won't need any sales closing techniques.

Your prospect will buy when she's ready to buy. And she will buy from you because you have earned her trust by providing unexpected free valuable information (newsletters, postal mail, and email) and perhaps even some free services.

By doing all this, you have kept your name continuously in front of your prospect. Simply by always being there, you have made it easier to buy from you than from someone else. Plus, people would much rather do business with someone they know than someone they don't know.

4. Getting the second sale

Those who buy from you a second time are 3-to-5 times more likely to keep buying from you than those who have bought from you only once. Someone who has bought from you only once cannot yet be considered a loyal customer. They are still testing the waters. I can almost always persuade someone to try something once—a restaurant for example. But if the restaurant is no good, there's very little I can say to persuade that unhappy person to return to that restaurant. Getting a second sale will depend on two factors: do they need the service or product again; and, most importantly, were they happy with the service or product they received from you the first time?

If your customer buys from you a second time, this means your customer was happy with the first purchase. You now have an opportunity to transform this customer into a loyal client, which is where your big money is made.

5. Deepening the relationship

We know it costs six times more to acquire a new customer than to keep an existing customer.

You have worked hard to acquire a customer. You should work equally hard to keep your customers. But most businesses invest far more money and energy trying to find new customers than making sure their existing customers are happy.

Your big money will always be made from your top 20 percent of your customers or clients. This is the well known 80/20 rule of marketing. The 80/20 rule is that 80 percent of your profit will come from the top 20 percent of your customers. The 80/20 rule, in fact, applies to just about all human behavior:

> ➢ 80% of America's wealth is created by 20% of the people
> ➢ 80% of commissions are earned by 20% of the salespeople
> ➢ 80% of your income is generated by 20% of your activities

I think the 80/20 rule should probably be renamed the 90/10 rule. If you were really to analyze this carefully, you would find that 90 percent of your profit likely comes from 10 percent of your customers. I like Starbucks coffee. I'll go in there maybe once every couple of weeks. But there are Starbucks fanatics who practically live there. These are the top 10 percent for Starbucks.

You want to create fanatics about you and your business. Like Starbucks, you want to cultivate this fanaticism. If not fanatics, you at least want to cultivate a class of champions who will not only buy from you faithfully, but who will recommend you to others, and who will serve as your unpaid sales force because they love you so much.

Most companies all but stop their marketing efforts upon acquiring the customer. They think their marketing job is over once the customer is in the door. They treat all customers about the same.

This is a terrible mistake.

Once the customer is acquired and has made a purchase, then the real marketing begins—the relationship building phase. The end goal of your marketing is not to find customers. That's just an intermediate step. The goal of your marketing is to find customers, transform customers into clients, then turn clients into champions for you. Of course, to do this your business must be worthy of being championed. More on this later.

Chapter Six

What we can learn from the Grateful Dead

"The relationship between the band and the Dead Heads must be nurtured because they are us and we are them."

—Phil Lesh
Base Player with the Grateful Dead

The Grateful Dead may be the most profitable rock band in history even though it has never had a #1 single or a #1 album.

Despite the death of its leader, Jerry Garcia, in 1995, Grateful Dead Productions continues to generate about $60 million a year in sales and licensing fees. Pretty good for a group that no longer exists.

Jerry Garcia and the Grateful Dead were among the greatest niche marketers in history. They never pursued the top spot on the pop charts—or any ranking on the pop charts. Instead, they dedicated themselves to pursuing a distinct style of music and cultivating a face-to-face relationship with their fans, building a loyal, even fanatical community of hundreds of thousands of Dead Heads by feeding this community exactly what it wanted—never deviating from its brand—for more than 35 years.

The Grateful Dead built its following by playing an average of more than 80 concerts a year for nearly four decades. As the years and decades rolled on, the Grateful Dead's following never waned, but actually strengthened. In the early 1990s, until Garcia's death in 1995, the Grateful Dead was probably the only band that could sell out major professional football stadiums on consecutive nights with no mass-market advertising.

Except for the fact that I'm a big fan of the Dead, I might never have known when the Grateful Dead was coming to Washington, D.C., because they did no mass-market advertising. But every summer when the Dead came into town, the 70,000 seats at RFK stadium would be sold out for both nights instantly, as soon as the tickets went on sale.

Unlike other rock bands, the Dead would allow the Dead Heads to record their concerts and even sell the bootlegged copies. In fact, a special area was set up at every concert specifically for the bootleggers, complete with sound equipment, so the recordings would be of decent quality.

Why would the band allow this?

They allowed it because a bootlegged copy of a concert was free advertising for the band. The band believed there was no better marketer of the band than its fans. So why not let them record the concerts and distribute the tapes even if the band did not receive one cent from the sale of the bootlegged tapes and CDs?

The Dead also made a decision to own every aspect of its band so it would have complete control over the production and marketing of its products. It did not want its product corrupted by traditional promoters and the big name recording labels. It put a ceiling on ticket prices, cracked down on scalpers, and did not mind at all if its hippie Dead Head fans made a few bucks by making their own Grateful Dead tie-dye shirts and products, even though not licensed by the band. It did not matter to the band that it made nothing on the "counterfeit" Grateful Dead T-shirts. The band just figured it was more free advertising.

Most importantly, the Dead made a decision to focus on its live concerts instead of recording records—because they were committed to spending face time with their fans. The Grateful Dead delivered more free concerts than any major rock band in history.

In so doing, they created a devoted community of hundreds of thousands of Dead Heads who followed them from concert to concert. You were not considered a Dead Head unless you had attended at least 100 Grateful Dead concerts. I've attended about 30.

There was also a kind of vague philosophy connecting the band and its Dead Head following. Their philosophy was intensely non-political and non-doctrinaire and went something like this: Everyone should love each other or at least be nice to each other; and if more people listened to music (presumably the Dead), the world would be a much happier, less angry, more peaceful place. Kind of a naive philosophy perhaps, but it certainly worked for its fans.

Jerry Garcia and the Dead did not care one wit about being at the top of the pop music charts. They cared about staying true to their unique style of folk rock music that had a touch of bluegrass and jazz underscored by a driving beat behind every song. They cared about their fans and giving their fans one song after another that had the unmistakable Grateful Dead beat and lengthy Jerry Garcia electric guitar riffs. And they turned their fans into a community.

As a result, the other bands, even the Beatles and Rolling Stones, have pretty well faded away. Young kids today don't listen to the Beatles or the Stones much. But the Grateful Dead brand remains strong. You'll see 14-year-old kids today wearing Grateful Dead tie-dye T-shirts because they think the Dead are "cool."

Harley Davidson motorcycles also follows this basic strategy, perhaps more consciously than the Dead. Harley-Davidson motorcycles are distinctly American road machines. They are big, noisy, and ride rough. They appeal to those who have a side to them that wish they could be like "Easy Rider," those who love the freedom of the road, who like to dress in black leather, who want to look like a Hells Angel—at least for a weekend. The Harley appeals a lot to former Vietnam War veterans.

On Memorial Day Weekend, we see 250,000 Harleys roar into Washington, D.C., as part of the annual "Rolling Thunder" event, aimed at honoring those who died in Vietnam, but also providing an opportunity for Harley riders to get together and party. Harley riders all feel themselves to be members of a community of fellow Harley riders.

You won't see many Yamahas at a "Rolling Thunder" or a Hells Angels gathering.

All of us niche target marketers can learn important lessons on how to create a unique brand and a loyal following by studying the Grateful Dead and Harley-Davidson. Their approach was not to be all things to all people. It was not to try to broaden their audience. It was to stay narrow and drill deep—to focus all attention on their most dedicated enthusiasts, to never take their following for granted, to keep feeding their customers more of what they want . . . and to ignore everyone else.

The Grateful Dead and Harley-Davidson stayed true to the 80/20 rule in marketing.

Chapter Seven
Avoid the price-cutting trap

So many companies fall into the trap of always trying to be cheaper than their competitors. You see ads all the time that say, "Best prices anywhere," or "If you can find this cheaper somewhere else, we'll pay you the difference plus 10%" or "plus 20%."

This is a big marketing mistake.

Never get into a discussion of which company—you or your competitor—has the lowest prices. Never get into a price war.

Price is certainly one factor your customers might consider when doing business with you. But price is not the only factor. In fact, price is one of the least important factors determining whether someone does business with you or not. You want clients who are primarily interested in quality, not price. So instead of focusing on how much you can afford to cut your price, focus instead on providing increased value to your customers.

A McKinsey study shows that a 1 percent cut in prices costs the average company 8 percent in profits. This means a 10 percent price cut wipes out 80 percent of the profit. This number varies depending on the industry you're in, but the point is that even a minimal price cut is often financially devastating. If your profit margin is 20 percent, a 10 percent price cut means you've just lost half your profit—half your income. But most businesses are operating on less than a 20 percent profit margin because they are in a constant price war with their competitors.

Now let's look at what happens when you raise your prices 10 percent.

So, if your profit margin was 20 percent, it's now 30 percent.

You have just increased your income by 50 percent with a 10 percent price increase that will hardly be noticed by your clients and customers. Everyone who's reading this chapter should raise their prices 10 percent right now. This is the fastest, easiest way to improve the profitability of your business.

With this 10 percent price increase, if you lost one-third of your customers, you would be just as profitable as you were before. Most likely, you won't lose any customers. In fact, increase your prices another 10 percent in six months, and see if you lose any customers. If you are a well-run business that provides excellent quality, service, and value, you'll be fine. So now you've doubled your profits in six months without adding a single new customer.

What people really want from you and your business

Never allow a conversation with your customers to focus on the issue of price. You don't want to do business with the bargain hunters and price shoppers anyway. These people are always more trouble than they're worth. They will drag you down. You are almost certain to lose money by servicing these customers.

If someone comes into your business and says, "I can get the same thing down the street for 10 or 20 percent less," your answer should be, "Then why are you here?"

Of course, the reason they are standing in front of you is they really can't get the same thing down the street for 20 percent less. They know you're the best. They want to do business with you. But they are scamming you. They are trying to frighten you into cutting your prices.

If people were really only interested in price, everyone would be driving the cheapest cars, wearing the cheapest clothes, drinking the cheapest wines, and living in the cheapest houses. When you think about it, the truth is, most people don't want the cheapest anything.

Do you want the cheapest surgeon operating on you? Do you want to fly on the plane that hires the cheapest pilots? Do you want the cheapest lawyer handling your important case? Do you want the cheapest teachers teaching your children? Do you want to stay in the cheapest motel, or watch the cheapest TV? Do you want the cheapest furniture in your home? Or the cheapest carpeting? Do you want your house painted with the cheapest paint? Do you want the cheapest roof? How about the cheapest electrical work and the cheapest plumbing you can find? Do you really want the cheapest haircut?

People want quality. People want great service. People want convenience, prestige, and a great customer experience. Most people understand they must pay a premium for these things. People also want a trusted relationship with those they do business with.

But here's another problem with getting caught in a price contest with your competitors.

If you keep cutting prices, soon you won't have enough profit to be able to provide the services your customers want and expect. You will find you have no choice but to start cutting corners and shaving your costs, or you'll go out of business. Soon your customers will start noticing the shoddier service and will leave anyway. Getting caught up in a price-cutting contest with your competitors is one of the surest roads to bankruptcy. Your customers won't appreciate your low prices, but they will blame you for shoddy service—shoddy service you can't help because your prices are too low.

You will never win a contest over who charges the least because there is always someone willing to do the work for less. There are lawyers out there who will work for $25 an hour. But do you want this lawyer? Isn't it likely that this $25-per-hour lawyer will end up costing you a whole lot more than you are saving if you had hired the best lawyer, the $300 per hour lawyer? This is what you want the discussion to be about.

There is only one reason people will pay a lawyer $300 or even $500 per hour—because they believe she's the best. They believe she's worth it. They believe the $500-per-hour lawyer is a better bargain, a better value than the $25-per-hour lawyer. They believe the $500-per-hour lawyer will ultimately save them a lot of money, or perhaps jail time. O.J. Simpson hired the Dream Team for a reason. Had he not, he likely would have ended up in the gas chamber. Those $1,000-per-hour lawyers were a bargain for O.J. These lawyers have no trouble getting work.

So refuse to get bogged down in a discussion of price with your customers and clients. Focus instead on the benefits you are providing. Focus on providing value, not cutting prices.

Of course, you must be well worth the prices you are charging.

How much should you charge?

Most businesses answer this question by figuring out how much it costs them to provide the service or product and then marking it up 15 percent or 20 percent.

If they find a cheaper way to provide the same service, they then cut their prices to stay in line with their lower cost of production.

Other companies look at what their competitors are charging and charge about the same. "Industry standard" is a phrase you hear a lot in certain fields when the subject of price comes up.

These are poor ways to set your prices.

The correct answer is: "You should charge what your customers are willing to pay."

What your customers will pay depends entirely on their perception of the value they are receiving.

If you bumped into Mozart at a local café, went up and introduced yourself, and then asked the great eighteenth century composer if he would mind writing a few lines of music on a paper napkin— and if he actually did it for you—how much might that napkin be worth?

It was very easy for Mozart to scribble a few lines of music on the napkin. Took him a few seconds. The napkin itself costs less than a penny. But that napkin might now be worth hundreds of thousands of dollars, or more. Why? Because there are people who will pay hundreds of thousands of dollars for this paper napkin . . . because they know it's a bargain.

I could scribble some music on a napkin also. It might look about the same, maybe look better than Mozart's scribbling. But I would not have much luck finding anyone to buy my scribblings. The difference between the napkin I scribble on and the napkin Mozart scribbles on is in the mind of the buyer.

Why do women want Gucci handbags? I myself think Gucci hand-bags look pretty crummy and cheap. The leather is thin and flimsy. Other far less expensive handbags are more durable and look better, at least to my eyes. About the only thing the Gucci handbag has going for it, in my estimation, is its staggeringly high price. But many women like Gucci handbags because the handbags are a status symbol. There are a lot of women who want people to know that they (or their husband or boyfriend) spent a lot of money to buy this handbag. Gucci is not really selling handbags. Gucci is selling status.

Who could have imagined people being willing to pay $3 for a cup of coffee at Starbucks when the Seven Eleven next door is selling the same size cup of perfectly good coffee for $1?

At 8:30 in the morning before work, Starbucks has a line going out the door of people waiting 20 minutes to buy its $3 cup of coffee, while not many are lining up for Seven-Eleven's coffee. I happen to like Seven-Eleven's coffee better. But apparently that's just me. Most people want Starbucks.

Is the Starbucks coffee really that much better than Seven-Eleven's?

I admit the Starbucks coffee is good, but I don't think it's 200% better than Seven-Eleven's. I think maybe it's 10% better, at most.

People are at Starbucks mostly for another reason—the experience.

Starbucks is selling more than coffee. Starbucks is selling a place where things are happening. For some, Starbucks is selling a social life. Some people spend all day at Starbucks, sitting in the easy chairs reading the paper and working on their laptop computer with their cup of coffee. Others sit at the café-style tables chatting with friends or hoping to meet a compatible member of the opposite sex. To some extent, Starbucks is also selling prestige and membership in an exclusive club. Blue collar workers drink Seven-Eleven coffee. The cool, young, hip crowd drinks Starbucks. Those who walk out of Starbucks with that distinctive Starbucks cup are, in effect, walking down a street with a status symbol, a piece of jewelry.

These are the reasons people are willing to pay $3 for a cup of coffee at Starbucks, but not at Seven-Eleven—not really because the coffee is that much better, or better at all. It's all in the marketing, in the positioning of the product in people's minds.

So, again, the answer to how much you charge is how much people are willing to pay. You can't charge a penny more. You are wounding yourself grievously if you charge less. You are literally giving money away if you are charging less than people are willing to pay.

Remember, you are not a charity. You are a business. You are in business to make a profit. Make your charitable work a separate activity, something you do outside your business.

So the correct phrasing of the question is not: "How much should I charge?"

The real question is: "How can I find out how much people are willing to pay?"

The short answer is: "Trial and error." In direct marketing we are always conducting price tests. Quite often we find that the higher price actually produces a higher rate of response, or no change in response rate at all.

Very often raising your prices actually improves the perception of your clients about you. You had to raise your prices because you are in so much demand. You are in so much demand because you are the best. Some people actually boast about paying their lawyer $500 per hour. Raising your prices can often help reposition yourself in the minds of your customers. We're no longer the cheap low-end service. We must charge more because we attend fanatically to every detail. We're perfectionists. We are involved in "The relentless pursuit of excellence," as Lexus tells us.

Of course, you must be ready to make good on this promise. Lexus will be in big trouble if its cars start falling apart or rattling as the vehicle trundles down the road.

But even before you undertake any new repositioning of yourself in the minds of your customers, which is a major task, you should almost certainly raise your prices 10 percent today, and then another 10 percent in six months. Then see what happens. If too many customers start walking out the door and if you have trouble finding new customers, you'll know you've raised your prices too much or too quickly.

I'm writing this chapter in 2005 when gasoline prices doubled in 12 months. But I'm not seeing a noticeable decline in the number of cars on the road. There will, of course, come a point when people will drive less. There will come a point when people start demanding alternative fuels. Will gas need to climb to $4 or $10 a gallon before that happens? Who knows exactly what that point is? Time and circumstances will tell us.

Your customers are almost certainly willing to pay more than you are now charging, even if you make no other change, even if you do nothing else this book recommends.

But the really big money is to get completely away from any discussion of price, to begin the process of repositioning yourself in the minds of your customers as the Lexus or Mercedes of what you do.

You don't want to market yourself as the cheapest doctor, the cheapest lawyer, the cheapest plumber, the cheapest hair salon, the cheapest mechanic, the cheapest seller of anything. You want to market yourself as the best—as Numero Uno in your field or your industry. Of course, you must be worthy of this positioning, which you will see is a recurring theme in this book.

Chapter Eight
Be a relentless collector of testimonials

Testimonials from your clients and customers are your single most powerful sales tool. Testimonials provide independent, third-party verification of your claims.

The most potent testimonials are not those that say how great you are, but testimonials that are mini-stories filled with details and specifics about all the great things you did for this customer or client.

And when your client is willing to give you a testimonial, don't just settle for printed copy. Ask your client for a digital audio recording of the testimonial that you can put on your Web site. If possible, get video of your clients' testimonials for featuring on your Web site. Printed words just sit on the page. But audio and video jump off the screen and give life to your Web site.

With today's technology, even a rank Internet beginner can turn her Web site into a powerful multi-media presentation, complete with video and audio testimonials from your, hopefully, ecstatic clients.

Video cams can fit in the palm of your hand. Take your video cam and digital recorder to meetings with your clients and ask for a full-blown multimedia testimonial. The best time to ask for a testimonial is right at the time your client is most pleased with your service. But even a grumpy client will often provide a glowing testimonial if asked.

The key is to never be shy about asking.

If you need to, you can suggest wording for your testimonials. But the testimonial will sound more genuine if it's in the customer's own words. A highly effective approach for collecting great testimonials is to interview your client with a video or audio recorder. Ask your client questions like:

1) Why did you choose to do business with us?

2) Describe your experience doing business with us.

3) What benefits did you see as a result of doing business with us?

4) How did we perform compared to other companies you've worked with who provide a similar service?

5) Were we easy to work with?

6) Do you think you will do business with us again?

These are just a few suggestions of the kinds of questions you could ask. Tailor your questions to fit your particular type of business and situation. If you have a conversation with your customer for up to 20 minutes on a video or audio recorder, you will then have plenty of material to edit and extract some wonderful testimonials for use on your Web site and in all your marketing materials.

Collecting testimonials should not be an afterthought. You can always use more testimonials. Make collecting customer and client testimonials on audio and video a major focus of your marketing strategy.

Chapter Nine

Turn your business into a "Referral Generation Factory"

The best lead is one that comes to you by way of a referral from an existing satisfied client.

This lead is already pre-sold on you by a credible third party who has nothing to gain from recommending you. Your lead has been sold on you by a trusted source—a friend or colleague who is having a great experience as your client. This is like a super-charged testimonial.

This chapter will show you how to systematize your referral generation and referral collection.

Here's some stunning referral math that should get you started today on building your "referral generation factory." When they give you referrals, think of your customers as actually replicating themselves.

If your customers can replicate themselves (by giving you referrals) at a rate of 2 new customers per year, you are literally growing at a rate of 200 percent per year minus your attrition rate.

Now, obviously, that's a growth rate that is not truly sustainable for long, or you would soon have the entire population of the world as customers. But it illustrates the power of making referrals the centerpiece of your lead generation strategy.

Let's take a more realistic goal. Let's say your existing customers replicate themselves at a rate of one new customer per year on average. And let's say your attrition rate is .7 customers per year. You are now growing at a rate of 30 percent per year.

Not bad. And these are very conservative numbers.

The way to speed up your growth is to increase the average number of referrals you are getting per customer and to reduce your attrition rate. If your business is well run, you should not have an attrition rate of .7 customers for every customer you have. And each of your customers, on average, should be able to produce more than one new customer a year for you.

Can you see the stunning potential of focusing your marketing efforts on generating referrals?

Set up a referral tracking system

As you build your referral system, there are five numbers you should track at a minimum. The numbers are:

> ➤ How many referrals are coming in each month?
>
> ➤ What sources are producing referrals and in what number?
>
> ➤ How many referrals are coming from your employees (by name)?
>
> ➤ How many referrals is it taking to produce a new customer?
>
> ➤ What is your customer attrition rate?

Create a referral mindset at your company

Post the referral numbers prominently in your company for every employee to see, perhaps in the reception area or in the main conference room. Create a referral scoreboard. Give bonuses and awards to employees who bring in the most referrals.

Remember, whatever you measure improves. Whatever you reward, you get more of. These are basic laws of human behavior and economics.

What's great about an entirely referral-based marketing strategy is that everyone in the company can and should be involved. With a referral-based marketing strategy, your marketing is not just run by a few specialists in the marketing department. Under this system, everyone becomes a marketer, and everyone is rewarded equally for bringing in referrals.

Have brainstorming meetings on how to make your referral program more productive. Make generating referrals a central focus of your company, from the chairman all the way down to the receptionist and janitor. Create a company of 100 percent sales and marketing people. Live and breathe referrals. Treat a referral as even more important than an actual sale, because referrals lead to sales. Referrals are a necessary precondition to a sale. Under this business model, there are no sales without referrals. Under this model, referrals are the lifeblood of the company.

Referrals are names that are poured into the top of the marketing funnel. After they've been put through your carefully-developed marketing process, which should be automatic, customers then fall out of the bottom of your marketing funnel and move into your customer cultivation program, which should also be automated, robotic.

From your customer cultivation program emerges repeat buyers who become loyal customers, and who then start generating more referrals. Your marketing and lead generation system literally becomes a perpetual motion lead generation factory that almost runs on its own.

The "Ask Method" of generating referrals

The primary method of generating referrals is so simple it's brilliant.

That method is simply to ask.

Ask your customers and clients for the names of three people who could benefit from your product or service. Three to six months later (whatever schedule you decide is best) ask this client for three more names. Make sure you have a set schedule for asking your clients for referrals. Whether it's every three months or every six months is up to you and is determined by what kind of clients they are and what your business is. Only you can know the answer, and some of this knowledge will be acquired through trial and error. If you are asking too often, your clients will let you know, in which case you back off a bit.

But almost certainly your problem is not that you are asking too often for referrals. Almost certainly your problem is that you are not asking enough, not asking regularly, and have no referral generation system in place at all.

Most of your very happy clients will be glad to provide good solid names for you.

When you get the names of prospects from your client, find out as much as you can about these leads. Ask your clients who they are, what kinds of business they are in and why they believe these people will benefit from your service or product. You need this information so you can write intelligently to these people.

When you write to your referred leads, your letter will read something like this:

> Dear Mrs. Smith,
>
> Your neighbor, Jeanne Cunningham, is a longtime client of Acme Pest Control.
>
> She suggested I contact you to let you know what we have been doing for her . . .
>
> *** Fill in details ***
>
> Because Mrs. Cunningham spoke so highly of you, I would like to meet you, inspect your home, and provide a free assessment of the possible pest situation in your home that you might not be aware of. Don't worry; I am not pressuring you to buy our service.
>
> I would just like to meet you, tell you what we do, and give you a free assessment of the possible pest situation in your home.
>
> I am also enrolling you in a free subscription to our monthly *Acme Pest Control Newsletter*, which is packed with valuable information on the pests that infest many of the homes in Great Falls, Virginia, largely unknown to the people living in these homes. These pests carry disease, intensify allergies, can permanently damage the structure of homes, and significantly reduce home values.
>
> To schedule your free assessment of the possible invisible pest situation in your home, please just return the enclosed postage-paid reply postcard, and I'll be in touch with you to schedule your free home pest assessment.

```
    Meanwhile, I will go ahead and enroll
you in a free subscription to the monthly
Acme Pest Control Newsletter unless you
tell me not to.

    Thank you so much for your time.  I
will look for your reply postcard to ar-
rive on my desk in the next few days.

            Sincerely,


            Richard Burr
            Chairman, Acme Pest Control, Inc.

P.S.  You might want to schedule your
free home assessment as soon as possible
because this month only we are offering
50% off on your first pest extermination
for first-time customers.  This offer ex-
pires on July 31.  I encourage you to ask
Mrs. Cunningham about her experience with
Acme Pest Control.
```

Can you see the power of this letter? This letter accomplishes five essential marketing steps:

1) You introduce your company.

2) You establish immediate credibility by mentioning Mrs. Cunningham, a respected neighbor and friend, as a satisfied customer.

3) You have an attractive offer that has a deadline, thus providing a reason to answer now.

4) You've painted a frightening and believable picture of the possible invisible pest situation that might be occurring right now in Mrs. Smith's home.

5) Even in the event that you receive no response, you've introduced your newsletter that will now start showing up monthly in Mrs. Smith's mailbox.

If Mrs. Smith does not respond immediately to your letter, she will likely call you the next time she sees a cockroach crawling across her counter. Your reply postcard should look something like this:

Postcard Reply

From: Mrs. Jill Smith

Richard,

[ ] Please contact me within the next 48 hours to schedule my free Pest Situation Home Assessment.

My phone number is _____

My email address is_____

[ ] To schedule my free assessment, I prefer you contact me by:

[ ] Phone   [ ] Email

[ ] Please enroll me in my free subscription to your monthly **ACME Pest Control Newsletter.**

If she responds, you now have all the contact information you need on Mrs. Smith to conduct your follow-up marketing campaign. But always remember, your marketing campaign should not include a barrage of heavy-handed sales pitches. Just keep feeding her valuable information. You want to be a welcome guest in her home, not an annoying pest. And you never want to be a source of embarrassment to those customers and clients who gave you the referral.

Your goal is to develop a trusted relationship. When Mrs. Smith needs pest control, she will call you. No Willie Loman-style sales pitch is ever needed.

As you can see, you can easily apply this method to almost any business. You will write your letter differently depending on what you are selling, who your leads are, and what kind of business you're in. A letter from a law firm to an executive of a large corporation would certainly sound and look different than a letter from a Pest Control company to a housewife.

But the method and system for contacting the lead and cultivating the business is exactly the same. For example, if writing to a referred lead about life insurance, you might begin your letter something like this:

```
Dear Mr. Smith,

    I was talking with your friend Steve Jones
yesterday and he mentioned to me that you might
need life insurance.

    Steve and I are long-time friends.  He is
also a life insurance policyholder of mine, has
been for more than 10 years.

    I would very much welcome meeting with you
to discuss your insurance situation.

    Even if you own some life insurance already,
I would like to talk with you about some recent
changes in the tax law that affect life insur-
ance -- changes that may require you to re-
structure some of your affairs to avoid a large
additional tax bite that you might not be an-
ticipating.

    We also have some very interesting new prod-
ucts that can allow you to protect your estate
and shelter a significant portion of your as-
sets from being taken by the IRS.

    I will be happy to meet with you at your
convenience, but the sooner the better.
```

```
    I can be reached anytime, either at my of-
fice number, which is _____ or on my cell
phone, which is _____.
```

```
    If I don't hear from you in the next few
days, I hope you won't mind if I give you a
call to see if we can schedule a meeting.
```

Can you see how much stronger a referred name is than simply writing to a cold name?

Not only is the referred name a qualified lead, because his friend knows he's looking for life insurance, or has a need for more life insurance. But your prospecting letter, even though you have never met this person, is attention-getting because the first line mentions the friend you both have in common. So you already have a bond, a connection. And the letter is far more credible, because your prospect can easily check with your friend to get your friend's assessment of you and your service.

Your client and friend, who you know is very happy with you, will say great things about you, further strengthening your marketing.

Does this ensure you will get a sale from this prospect? Of course not, but the odds are now exponentially more in your favor.

Regardless of whether you get the meeting this time, you have an "in" now to add this lead to your mailing list. This prospect starts getting your informative and interesting newsletters on life insurance and other financial matters. When and if he ever starts thinking about needing more life insurance, the odds are he'll want to talk with you.

As with all your marketing, you will never pressure anyone into buying life insurance if they don't want it, and don't think they need it. Your goal as a marketer is to be at the top of the list at the exact moment your prospect starts thinking he might need or want your service.

This referral strategy can be replicated over and over again. The more clients you have, the more referrals you can collect and mail. The key is simply to ask your happy clients for the names of others they know who can use your service.

Can marketing and sales really ever get easier and more simple than this? As the Nike commercial says, "Just do it."

IMPORTANT: In all your marketing materials, be sure to prominently display your phone number, physical address, and Web site address. I'm amazed at how many businesses forget this seemingly obvious detail. In all your marketing, you want to make it as easy and as convenient as possible for people to find you and do business with you.

The "Explain Method" of generating referrals

Your best clients will refer people to you automatically if you instill in them a referral mindset, just like you're doing with all your employees.

In your newsletters and marketing materials, always explain that you are a referral-based business, that you invest the company's money in serving clients, not in expensive advertising. Your clients will understand and appreciate this information.

When a referred lead or customer comes in the door, reward the source of the referral with a nice gift—perhaps a set of luggage tags, a flower arrangement, a jar of honey, a T-shirt, a nice pen, anything thoughtful that will show your appreciation. There's no need for an expensive gift. Not only will your thank-you gift reinforce your existing customer's loyalty to you by reminding her that you are a quality, thoughtful company that takes no customer for granted, but you are instilling a referral mindset in your customer base.

For your best clients, there's no need to pay them a commission for a referral. This just cheapens the referral. Your best clients will be happy to keep sending referrals to you if they are having a happy client experience with you. Your best clients are your unpaid sales force. And they are far better than any salespeople you could ever pay.

Are you worthy of referral?

No referral strategy will work if you are not worthy of referral.

Are you delivering on your promises? Are you delivering on time? Are you exceeding the expectations of your customers, or merely meeting expectations? Are you thanking your customers for their business, and doing so in creative, thoughtful ways? Is your product or service superior to your competitors'? Are you fanatical about the details of your work? Can you honestly say your company, like the Lexus slogan, is about the "relentless pursuit of excellence?"

If your answer to any of these questions is "no," then you and your company are probably not worthy of referral.

Do you recommend movies or restaurants that are simply okay, that merely met your expectations and nothing more? Probably not. You recommend movies and restaurants that caused you to say "Wow! That was great!"

Are you causing your customers and clients to say "Wow!"?

If not, your referral program will not work.

This is why every function in your company is a marketing function.

And this is why everyone working in your company must think of themselves as marketing people first.

Marketing people think first about what the customer needs—not what the company needs. Marketing people think first about how to solve the customer's problem, not how to solve their own problem. The Ritz-Carlton has given every employee *carte blanche* authority, no questions asked, to spend up to $2,000 of the hotel's money to fix whatever problem a customer is complaining about. At the Ritz-Carlton, every employee is a marketer, which means every employee is trained to serve the customer first.

That's why the Ritz-Carlton is the Ritz-Carlton.

Instill this mindset in every employee, and your company will be worthy of referral.

Paying for referrals

Pay bonuses for referrals and commissions to staff when referrals turn into customers. When your staff brings in business, pay them the same bonuses and commissions that you pay your sales people. You'll find out who your real salespeople are.

I am befuddled when the green eyed-shade people in companies cut the commissions of salespeople who are making "too much" money in their estimation. The best salespeople should have their commissions raised, not lowered. In the most successful companies, the best salespeople are the best paid of anyone. The best salespeople usually make more than the president or chairman of the company.

There is no faster way to bring down the morale of your sales force than to start nickel and diming them on their commissions. If your top salesperson is making $1,000,000 in commissions a year, you should be ecstatic because this means your company is doing great. You should raise this salesperson's commission as a reward for great service to the company.

Bring a friend

A great way to generate referrals is to offer the source of the referral something free.

If you bring a friend to my deli, your lunch is free. If you bring a friend to my hair salon, your haircut is free. If you bring a friend who signs up for a gym membership, your membership is free for the next three months. If your referral becomes a customer, we'll give you two weeks of free lawn care. In the right kinds of businesses, offers like these will generate an avalanche of new business.

Never forget to track every aspect of your referral system. And always test different offers aimed at attracting referrals.

TEST, TRACK, and SYSTEMATIZE. These are the three most important words in marketing.

Nominations combined with an appeal to prestige, exclusivity, and achievement

I'm a member of a public policy organization called the Council for National Policy that meets three times a year in nice locations around the country—Boca Raton, Aspen, Laguna Beach, places like that. The purpose of the organization is to connect successful business leaders with right-of-center public policy organizations and candidates.

The goal is to interest these business leaders and wealthy individuals in politics and public policy and to get them contributing money to these non-profit public policy organizations, as well as mostly Republican candidates. The only way you can join this organization is to be nominated first by another member.

You then have the privilege of paying a $2,500 membership fee every year, plus the fee for attending the three meetings. At these meetings you might hear from the President or Vice President of the United States, the Speaker of the House, the Senate Majority Leader, and many other political leaders and luminaries. The attraction of membership in the Council is you will have plenty of opportunity to meet with and talk with Republican Party leaders and other influential people. The Council is marketed as an exclusive organization. It's considered an honor to be invited to join.

I'm not sure it is an honor. But that's how it's sold. And the only way you can get in is with a referral from another member. You will then receive a letter announcing that you have been nominated for membership in the Council by so and so.

This strategy can be deployed effectively for all kinds of organizations and associations.

One of my clients is a creator of educational programs for high-achieving young people. The way we find students is to write to teachers and ask them to nominate six of their best students to participate in this prestigious National Young Leaders Conference.

The nominations come in from the teachers. The names and addresses of the student nominees are entered into a computer database. The nominees then receive a letter that begins something like this:

> Congratulations!
>
> I am pleased to announce that you have been nominated to be a National Scholar and Delegate to _____ in Washington, D.C., this fall.
>
> Your teacher, [Name], identified you as one of her most outstanding students. The Nominations Committee then examined your academic record and concluded that you qualify for nomination.
>
> You should feel proud of your exemplary academic record and your selection to be a National Scholar representing the state of Virginia.

This letter is sent out in an impressive-looking invitation holder. The package looks a lot like a wedding invitation. It includes a program schedule, an impressive list of advisors, even a short form letter from President Bush welcoming the students, and an Enrollment Application. Another letter is sent to the parents at the same time. The tuition for the five-day conference is about $1,400.

The point is, this list is developed by way of a referral strategy. The students are found by asking teachers to provide the names of (nominate) their best students. This is how the prospect (invitation) list is built.

When this letter arrives, it has instant credibility because the teacher's name is mentioned right away. If this child's teacher is involved in this program, it must be worthwhile. This will be very powerful evidence for the parent of the value of the program.

This is a potent way to use the referral strategy, and works well for offers designed to appeal to the desire for exclusivity and prestige.

Strategic alliances

Form strategic alliances with vendors and companies that are in your industry, but aren't direct competitors. For example, I have a strategic alliance with a great mailshop called RST Marketing.

Mailshops are not printers (though some also print). Mailshops are companies that take printed material, collate it, insert it all into envelopes, affix postage, and mail it. Mailshops are a critical vendor for large direct mail programs. RST specializes in producing highly-personalized, high-impact mailings that don't look mass-produced. That's RST's niche.

Not only does RST produce all my high-end, highly personalized direct mail pieces, but I send others to RST, and RST sends its clients to me if they need copywriting, creative work, or marketing strategy. If RST and I do a project together, we sometimes share in the profit.

RST has a sales force that also acts as a sales force for me. If a prospect says, yes, we need a mailshop, but we first need a package to mail—meaning a letter written and a package designed—RST says we can do that too, through Ben Hart. It becomes a "win-win" relationship for both RST and me, because RST is not in the sales letter-writing business and I'm not in the mailshop business. We need each other.

Sit down with a pencil and paper and write down strategic alliances that would work for both you and another company.

For a strategic alliance to work, it's usually best if the two companies work in different areas of the same field or industry, where there are opportunities to combine efforts to create a whole that is more profitable for both parties than the services would be if sold separately. A direct mail marketer needs printing, a mailshop, a list company, a copywriter, and graphic design. Very often these services are provided by different companies. This opens up tremendous opportunities for a strategic alliance. A strategic alliance can function like a breeder reactor, generating great business for everyone.

Strategic alliances vastly improve overall marketing because no prospect feels they are being sold an entire package, such as with a one-stop shop agency. When RST says, "You want Ben Hart doing your copywriting and creative work," this comes across as an unbiased recommendation, not a sales pitch. I'm assuming RST truly believes I'm good at what I do just as I honestly believe RST is the best at what it does. A strategic alliance expands your capabilities and makes you seem a lot bigger than you really are. Plus, you don't have the burden of a lot of permanent added overhead.

A strategic alliance is not a partnership or a marriage. It can be informal most of the time, or deals can be formalized for certain distinct projects and ventures. I'm a big fan of strategic alliances as a vehicle for generating more business for everyone involved.

Ask friendly competitors for overflow work

I'm friends with all of my competitors.

I don't really consider them to be competitors at all. The truth is, there's enough business out there for everyone. I like my competitors because they do what I do. We share the same interests.

When we get together, we share our secrets and our battle stories. We have a great time. I love my competitors because we have the same problems, challenges, and interests.

In whatever business we're in, there are the Top Dogs and there are those who are just starting out. Those who are just starting out are not a threat to the Top Dogs. The Top Dogs almost always have an overflow of business that they reject because it's not profitable enough.

If you are just getting established, ask the Top Dogs in your industry for their overflow work.

Form a strategic alliance with them. Encourage your Top Dog competitor not to turn down the work, but to allow you to do the work as a subcontractor. If the Top Dog charges $250 per hour, offer to do the job for $150 per hour (if that makes economic sense for you). Allow the Top Dog firm to invoice at their usual rate, pay you the $150 per hour you've agreed to and let the Top Dog firm keep the $100 profit for doing almost no work except the invoicing—work the Top Dog firm was going to turn down.

Again, this is "win-win" for everyone.

The client wins because they get the work done.

The Top Dog firm wins because it gets $100 of the $250 per hour it charges for your time, while having to do next to no work for the fee. Most importantly, the Top Dog firm does not annoy a customer by rejecting the work.

And you win because you make your usual $150 per hour.

Or if you are the Top Dog, don't be afraid to help out your start-up competitor. If you can keep a client happy by subcontracting with your start-up competitor, and make a little money along the way, do it. Your customer will be pleased that you always have time for her work, even during your busiest times. There's no need to see your competitors as adversaries. There's more business out there than any of us can handle. Work together intelligently and creatively to create a bigger pie and more business for everyone.

Chapter Ten

How to generate leads . . . other than with referrals

Salespeople will not survive long if they are told to generate their own leads through cold calling. They will get discouraged, psychologically and emotionally worn down by all the rejections. Salespeople need leads. And they need good leads. Or you will lose your sales force.

If someone calls your office in answer to one of your lead generation letters, the chances are you've got a good lead. You have someone who's interested. You have someone who wants to talk. You have someone who has called you on his schedule, who is eager to chat, who is not being interrupted at the dinner hour by a telemarketer.

All calls that come into your office in answer to your letter are at least 10 times more likely to buy than a "cold call" prospect who wasn't looking for you and has never heard of you.

There are three basic categories of lead generation programs:

1. Business-to-consumer

The practicality of lead generation programs to consumers is dictated almost entirely by price point. Lead generation programs make economic sense if you are selling big-ticket items, such as homes, mortgages, vacations, vehicles, landscaping, lawn care, legal services, insurance, or country club memberships. Lead generation programs to consumers probably won't make sense for items under $50. For low-cost items (books, magazine subscriptions, kitchen gadgets, and the like) the mailing will likely need to do all the selling.

When selling low-cost or low-margin items, it just becomes too costly to come at the prospect over and over again to get the sale, unless you have a lot of money to spend and can wait a long time to recover your investment.

A potentially cheap way to generate leads for your mailings to consumers is through the Internet. With the Internet, you don't have postage costs, paper costs, or printing costs. Internet marketing is different from direct mail in that, with direct mail, your mailing reaches out to the consumer—actually gets into their home.

You can't do that on the Internet.

With the Internet you have to learn how to put bait out there. Your leads then must find you. Direct mail is more like hunting. With direct mail you go out and get the customer. You physically find the customer and drag him in the door, like slaying a wildebeast. Internet marketing is more like fishing. You put your hook and bait in the water, and you wait for your customers and leads to come to you. And they will come if you have the right bait.

The Internet can be a wonderful lead generation tool if used skillfully.

2. Business-to-business

Lead generation programs should be a major feature of just about any marketing campaign directed toward business. Nearly everything a business buys is almost by definition a big-ticket item.

Businesses buy even paper, pens, and paper clips in bulk. So it's well worth investing a significant sum of money to land a successful business as a client or customer.

3. Public relations-generated leads

This category is outside the scope of this book, but I'll mention it in passing. These are leads generated by news coverage and articles. People read about you in the *Wall Street Journal* and call, write, or track you down on the Internet. Free news coverage can produce a flood of leads and even orders. But I'm not covering it much here because this is a book about measurable, predictable marketing that you can systematize, not public relations campaigns, which are a different animal.

Generating news coverage is difficult to systematize and control. It's great when it happens, and there are steps you can take to increase the odds of receiving news coverage, but it's difficult to control or predict. So that's all I'll say about public relations here.

Some facts about "lead generation" that should inspire you

Here is some data that might whet your appetite for putting in place a lead generation strategy immediately:

o About 60% of all inquiries are made with the intention of buying your product or a similar product from your competitor. The question for these folks is not whether they will buy, but from whom will they buy.

o 53% of those inquirers who contact you will also contact your competitor.

o 25% of those who have an "immediate need" will buy from the company that triggered the call with a mailing or advertisement.

o 20% of those who inquire and ask for information never receive any information. No one from the company ever follows up.

o Of those companies that do follow-up with information to the inquirer, 43% deliver the information too late to be of any use.

o 59% of inquirers say they threw away the information they received because it had nothing to do with why they had inquired and so was of no use.

o About 10% of inquiries are considered "hot leads"—meaning people who will buy immediately, either from you or your competitor.

These statistics, provided by the Advertising Research Foundation, should encourage you in two ways. This data illustrates the enormous potential profitability of a lead generation program, and also reveals how inept most companies are at following up leads quickly.

The Lesson: If you launch a lead generation program, make sure you are set up to immediately answer and fulfill requests. Have your follow-up letters and packets ready. Make sure your sales team is ready to swing into action.

Feeding your sales force qualified leads

What's worse: too many leads or not enough?

That's really not the right question. The correct question is: "What is a qualified lead?" or "How do I assess the quality of the lead?"

It's easy to generate inquiries. That's no problem at all. If I put out an ad that says "Free Sex! Call 1.800_____," I will get lots of calls, lots of interest—including, probably, from the police.

What your sales force wants are good leads—leads that have a real chance of buying. Nothing will discourage your sales team more than feeding them a lot of bad leads. The challenge is generating *qualified* inquiries.

One way to qualify a lead is not to bury the price of your product. Don't put the high price in a bright red banner headline. But include it somewhere in the literature you are sending, if there's a fixed price.

That way you will know those who answer your letter are not discouraged about the price. They are qualified leads.

If mentioning the price is not possible because of the nature of your service or business, another way to qualify your leads is to know who you are sending your lead generation letters to. You only write to those who can afford you, who are used to paying what you charge. The question then is not whether the prospect can afford you, but whether the prospect needs your service.

I will then use some kind of reply device the prospect would need to return to become qualified for a sales call:

Such a lead generation letter might look something like this:

```
     If I could show you how I can save you 20%
over what you are paying now for your printing,
would you be interested in meeting with me?
```

   If your answer is yes, please return the enclosed reply card and I will call to set up a
meeting.

   The reason I am confident we can cut 20% off
what you are paying now for your printing is
because I know exactly what our competitors are
charging.

   Please be assured that our lower prices in no
way mean lower quality. Quite the opposite.

   Because we have just refitted our entire plant
with brand new state of the art web presses, your
printing will always be crisp and clear. In
fact, if you ever find a problem with the quality
of our printing, we'll print it again for you at
no charge.

   I am very much hoping you will give us a
chance to bid on your business.

   I am anxious to receive your answer by return
mail in the next few days.

        Sincerely,

        John Q. Sample
        Vice President of Customer Service
        Brand X Printing

P.S. The companies we've been meeting with are
stunned by our low prices. As a result, our
printing press schedule is nearly full. So it's
important we meet soon, within the next week if
possible, before we are completely booked.

If you are not able to meet with me, I will be
very happy to meet with the person who makes the
decisions about your printing. In that case,
please just write the name of the person I should
talk with on the enclosed reply card and mail it
back to me. You can also call me at **1.800** _____.
Thank you so much.

Anyone who answers this letter is a great prospect. The conversation is started. The relationship has begun.

Notice that the letter does not promise a follow-up call in the event the reader does not respond. That's because the purpose of this letter is to qualify the lead. Of course, this letter does not rule out a follow-up call either.

If the reply card is returned, you might not get an order right away, but you have the green light to schedule a meeting. And you have an opening to continue to send your prospect follow-up letters, information, announcements, invitations to social events, email communications, a newsletter, baseball tickets, whatever seems appropriate.

The main thing is to keep the conversation going and to stay in front of your prospect. You now have a better-than-even chance of getting some business. And if your quality is good and if you keep your promises, you might be able to lock in another big account.

Follow-up your letter with a call

You will be far more successful with your lead generation and sales calls if you send a letter before you call. That way you are not a total stranger when your call comes in asking for a meeting.

One of the biggest mistakes marketers and sales people make is to rely on one shot—one letter or one call. The big advertisers (Nike, McDonald's, Coke) know they must be in front of their market all the time. If you watch an hour of golf or basketball, you might see ten Nike ads. You must keep yourself in front of your prospects continuously with interesting letters, emails, newsletters, faxes, or announcements.

When they need your service, you want to be right there when they are making their decision.

Give away a free sandwich

Throughout this book you will see a recurring theme.

Never be afraid to give away some of what you do for free. So many businesses boast to me that "We never give away anything for free. To do so would be to cheapen our product."

What a blunder! What idiocy!

One way or another, you will have to pay for customers. You will have to pay for advertising and marketing. Orders and customers do not just show up on their own. You have to find them. You have to go out and get them. This costs money.

Giving away some of what you do free is the cheapest form of advertising. It's the cheapest way to quickly and immediately show your prospects what you do and how good your service or your product is. I would never buy a software program without a "free trial." I want to test drive the software. I would never buy a car without a "free test drive."

Let's say you've just opened up a new deli in an office building. Why not distribute a flier to every office in the building, perhaps in neighboring office buildings as well, and offer a free sandwich to anyone who comes in before Tuesday, June 1?

Those who come in for the free sandwich will also buy a soda, a bag of chips, a cookie, maybe a cup of coffee. So you aren't losing much. And if your sandwiches are great, you are gaining customers who will come back many, many times.

This is very cheap marketing. And I can't think of a better way to sell a deli.

When I was a young direct mail copywriter trying to land a client, I would offer my prospect a risk-free mailing. If the mailing failed, the client would owe nothing. An offer like this requires a good deal of confidence that the mailing will work because even test mailings are expensive—often costing thousands of dollars. But I should not be in the business if I don't think my mailings will work.

But here's the calculation I make: If just one in five of my mailings work, this is successful . . . because test mailings are relatively small compared to rollouts of successful tests. And if a test works, the upside can be to mail millions of letters, sometimes tens of millions.

So don't be afraid to let your prospects sample what you do for free.

If your product or service is great, you won't lose money . . . you'll gain customers. Give away a free trial subscription, free perfume, a free newsletter, a free stock tip, a free special report, a free mailing, free coffee, a free pastry, a free test-drive, a free lesson, a free seminar, free beer, a free wine tasting, a free cigar. It's an offer no intelligent person can refuse. And it's likely your cheapest form of marketing.

Generate store traffic

Bookstores love to bring in a famous author with a new bestselling book for a book signing and maybe have her give a lecture. The author loves it because it helps sell her new book. The bookstore loves it because it brings people into the store. Stores rely on traffic to generate business because most people in stores buy on impulse.

Creating attractive events is one of the best methods to generate traffic in your store. If you are an art gallery, have a free wine and cheese reception with a famous artist.

Here's a concept for a dealer in high-end cars:

You are cordially invited
to the
Annual Lexus Driving Exposition

You can test drive all our 2007 models
on our specially designed driving course.

Then cap off this extraordinary experience with
free golf tips from PGA pro John Daly
or a luxurious spa treatment.

September 9, 2006
9:00 a.m. to 6:00 p.m.

Free wine and cheese reception at 4:00 p.m.

This could generate some great store traffic for a Lexus dealer, and could be especially effective mailed to prospects whose current car leases are on the verge of expiring.

Hold a seminar

Holding a seminar in your area of expertise can be a potent method of generating interest in your business, red-hot leads, and clients. This approach can work well for financial planners; plastic surgeons; nutrition, wellness, health, and medical centers; wealth-building programs; real estate; sales and marketing programs; business leadership and management; and other fields where specialized knowledge and expertise are at a premium.

I've gained many clients from those who heard a speech I delivered or who attended a seminar I conducted.

There seems to be an almost unlimited market for educational programs. People crave knowledge and information because gaining knowledge and information in your field is the key to getting where you want to go in life. Knowledge is power. Yes, it's a cliché; it's also true.

Chapter Eleven

Make your marketing robotic, automatic, and hands-free

The free 24-hour recorded message hotline

The "24-Hour Free Recorded Message Hotline" is a great tool you need to create your automatic, robotic, hands-free marketing system that runs itself.

And it's very low-tech. No technology whatsoever to learn.

You should include your toll-free 1.800 number Free 24-Hour Recorded Message Hotline in all your advertising and marketing. The Free 24-Hour Recorded Message Hotline is your sales presentation.

But, as with 90 percent of your marketing under this system, it is not advertised as a sales pitch. It's advertised as unbiased information for the consumer. Ads promoting your 24-Hour Free Recorded Message should read like this:

Sample realtor ad:

"The Seven Most Common Mistakes People Make When Buying a Home"
Call now to get your free Buyer's Guide

Free 24-Hour Recorded Message Hotline
1.800_____

Sample financial planner ad:

> ## "The Five Worst Financial Planning Mistakes"
> Call now to get your free step-by-step guide to successful financial planning
>
> ## Free 24-Hour Recorded Message Hotline
> ## 1.800_____

Sample pest control company ad:

> ## "The Seven Disease-Carrying Pests that are Probably Infesting Your Home"
> Call now to get your free Consumer Survival Guide
> ## Free 24-Hour Recorded Message Hotline
> ## 1.800_____

Sample home builder ad:

> ## "The 11 Tricks Some Unethical Home Builders Use to Steal Your Money"
> Call now to get your free Consumer Protection Guide
> ## Free 24-Hour Recorded Message Hotline
> ## 1.800 _____

Sample ad for plastic surgeon:

> ## "Don't Have Plastic Surgery Until You've Read this Consumer Protection Report"
>
> **Call now to get your free Consumer Awareness Guide**
> ### Free 24-Hour Recorded Message Hotline
> ### 1.800_____

Sample ad for law firm:

> ## "The Nine Most Common Mistakes People Make When Hiring a Lawyer"
>
> **Call now to get your free Consumer Awareness Guide**
> ### Free 24-Hour Recorded Message Hotline
> ### 1.800 _____

Sample ad for other service company:

> ## "How to Hire an Ethical _____"
>
> **Call now to get your free Buyer's Guide**
> ### Free 24-Hour Recorded Message Hotline
> ### 1.800 _____

Notice the pattern of these ads. The headlines either tap into an existing fear or create a fear or anxiety (a fear they did not know they should have before now). This fear compels readers of these headlines to call for their free "Consumer Protection Guide" or special report to find out what mistakes to avoid, what the most common scams are in the industry, or the threats consumers face if they don't act now.

Remember, "fear" is the #1 motivator triggering people to buy. In the words of the great advertising pioneer David Ogilvy, "You must first show the fire before you try to sell fire extinguishers." You must outline the threat, the danger, the crisis before you sell a solution to the problem.

And you do this not with a lot of empty hype words that so many advertisers use. You do this with facts and proof. That's why it is so powerful to offer a free Consumer Protection Guide or a free Consumer's Research Report on the subject of interest to your prospect.

Notice also that the ad says the message is recorded.

Contrary to what you might expect, people are more likely to call a recording because they know they aren't going to be subjected to a high-pressure pitch from a desperate salesman. They can listen for as long as they want and hang up if they choose, without concern for being rude.

But how do you know you are reaching those who want this service?

Because you advertise in places where you know people are looking who want this service, such as the Yellow Pages, or sections of newspapers where all your competitors are running their ads. In fact, a great way to figure out where to run your ads is to find out where your competitors are advertising. For certain kinds of businesses, don't overlook classified ads.

As with all direct marketing, you will always want to start small with each advertising source and test. You want to test ads and test sources. Your ad might be great, but if it's appearing in the wrong place, it won't work. Conversely, the ad won't work anywhere if it's no good. Follow the copy guidelines in the ads I've written above, and you'll be on the right track. But it will be up to you to find the right places to run your ads.

The surest approach is to rely on the research your competitors have already done for you. Run your ads where they are running their ads. They run ads in those places because they've found they work. As you get rolling, you will think of other places to test-run your ads. But don't be a pioneer yet. Travel down the well-beaten paths your competitors have already cut for you.

Here's the beauty of these ads. They are short and therefore will cost you very little money when you run them in the Yellow Pages, in your local newspaper, in classified ads, in magazines.

You can also put this ad on fliers you distribute, on your business card and, of course, on your Web site, prominently displayed.

These ads are attention-getting. These ads don't look like other ads in the Yellow Pages. They look almost like consumer protection public service ads, published to alert consumers to costly and damaging mistakes people almost always make if they don't know about them.

People then call to hear your "Free 24-Hour Hotline" 1.800 number message.

Your recorded message can give many of the highlights of the free Consumer Protection Guide you are offering, such as "How to avoid homebuilder scams" (if you are in the homebuilding business). In addition, your message tells your listener what your company does.

You deliver your offer—let's say a free assessment of the pest situation in the prospect's home (if you're a pest control company). If your listener found your ad in the Yellow Pages, chances are she wants the service you are offering right now. So it's fine for your Recorded Message to make your basic sales pitch. A free assessment, a free analysis, a free consultation, 50 percent off for first-time customers are potent offers to bring in new buyers.

Free Recorded Messages are great places for your audio testimonials, listings of your impressive clients and track-record of achievements. But be careful not to spend much time talking about you. Ninety percent of what you say must be about what you will do for your listener. Stress benefits to the listener, and the dangers of not acting now. It's fine if your Free 24-Hour Recorded Message is long, if what you have to say is interesting. In advertising, the longer your prospect listens to you, the better chance you have for the sale. So your 24-Hour Recorded Message can be 10 minutes or longer, if what you have to say is fascinating.

Especially important is to stress your super-charged guarantee and your irresistible offer for first-time customers that no intelligent person looking for such a service can possibly refuse. "Free trial" and "free for first-time buyers" is always a powerful offer.

At any moment, the listener can click out of the sales pitch and order the free Consumer Protection Guide you've offered and, hopefully, also the free consultation or analysis or free trial or free initial service you are also offering. The listener can press a key to be connected directly to you or a live sales person if it's during business hours or press another number to leave a message on voice mail. You now have a hot prospect.

You must now follow-up immediately, or your prospect will find the service somewhere else. This is absolutely essential because you are providing exactly the service she's clearly searching for. This is money hanging on a tree that is simply waiting to be collected.

And you did no work to get this hot prospect. Once the system is set up, it works on its own, automatically and hands-free. It works while you sleep. It works while you are on vacation. Your 24-Hour Recorded Message is your unpaid sales force that never gets tired, never gets discouraged, never calls in sick, and works for you all the time, 24/7.

You just need to be ready to handle all the business that will pour in.

You can set up your Free 24-Hour Recorded Message Hotline in one of two ways:

1. **The unsophisticated** (but still effective) way is to call your phone company and set up a voice mailbox. Be sure you have caller ID that will allow you to capture many names and phone numbers of callers, including those who hang-up and leave no message. These are still leads, though not nearly as qualified as those who leave a message.

2. **The better,** more sophisticated way is to hire a company that understands this process and is in business for exactly this purpose. Just like there are companies that are in business to provide auto-response email, there are companies that are in business to provide "Free 24-Hour Recorded Message Hotlines" for your prospects and customers to call—companies that understand marketing and what you are attempting to achieve. The company I use for this is Automatic Response Technologies, Inc., (ART) at: **www.automaticresponse.com**.

This company will teach you step-by-step how to set up your 24-Hour Recorded Message Hotlines and show you how to use this tool to maximize the effectiveness of your lead generation program. In addition, this company has a voice broadcast service that allows you to deliver audio messages to your email list.

With ART's system, your leads will never receive a busy signal because an unlimited number of prospects can call at the same time to hear your message. And ART will automatically capture names, phone numbers, and even physical street addresses of many of your callers, including those that hang up and leave no message for you.

In addition, you can have any number of recorded messages tailored for different products and services you might be offering. And you can quickly and easily test different messages and advertising media with campaigns running side-by-side.

An actual voice is so much more powerful than print. A bond starts to form as the listener hears more of what you have to say. People want to do business with people, not with a printed page. People want a relationship with those they do business with. You have a much greater chance of achieving this with a detailed, recorded presentation in your own voice. You are, in effect, conducting a seminar for your listeners. You are marketing by providing information. You are marketing by educating.

The recorded message, of the type I am describing, is the next best thing to standing in someone's living room and having a one-on-one conversation.

But you are doing it automatically and robotically, while you are sleeping, while you are playing tennis, while you are watching the football game or playing with your kids. You'll never need to make your introductory sales pitch again. Instead, you'll just send prospects to your "Free 24-Hour Recorded Message Hotline" to hear your sales presentation . . . over and over and over again.

The machine is now doing Willie Loman's job from Arthur Miller's tragic play *Death of a Salesman*. The machine delivers a perfect sales presentation every time. The machine never gets tired. The machine is always cheery and upbeat. The machine never gets discouraged. The machine never gets beaten down by rejection after rejection. The machine doesn't require a salary or benefits. The machine doesn't need to be reprimanded for being late to work or cajoled to keep working for you. The machine doesn't require a desk, chair, or computer. The machine doesn't require motivation speeches or training. The machine just keeps making your introductory sales presentation perfectly all the time, 24/7, forever.

This, in fact, is how you want all your marketing to function. And it can—if you set up the system correctly.

Depending on the product or service you are offering, you might test whether to include in your ad a Web site address leading your reader to a landing page that requires her to fill out a form to receive your free Consumer Protection Guide. As a general rule, I don't like this approach, but it depends.

If you are advertising in the Yellow Pages, people looking there want the service now. People who want service now use the phone. People surfing the Internet are more nibblers. They are researching the subject but are usually not in need of instant emergency service. Those who grab the Yellow Pages want service now.

But if you are running banner ads on Web sites related to your product or service, you'll want your banner ad to link to your site, most likely a landing page. You would then display your 24-Hour Recorded Message there, on your site, on the landing page, perhaps throughout your site.

As with all marketing tools, you must use the tool that fits the task at hand. A saw is a great tool, but not for hammering nails.

The folks who are calling your "24-Hour Free Recorded Message Hotline" are usually people who want service now. When someone picks up the phone and calls, they are serious. The phone is a "need it now" tool. The Internet is used by researchers, dabblers, nibblers. They are thinking about it and will get back to us when they are ready. With all marketing, but especially with the Internet, your job is to find a way to capture email address of those who are interested in what you are doing. And then develop a program that will keep you and your service in front of that person so that when the prospect is ready, the prospect thinks of you first.

Of course, these are general observations based on my own experience. There are differing patterns of response depending on the product you are selling. As with all your marketing media and tools, you must always TEST, TEST, TEST.

As you get to know me, I will sound like a broken record on the importance of testing.

How to use traditional advertising media

You no longer need to buy large expensive display ads in newspapers, magazines, or the Yellow Pages. All you need to do is drive people to your "Free 24-Hour Recorded Message Hotline" or to your Web site to order and download their free special report, book, or Consumer Protection Guide—or whatever it is you are offering free.

Your recorded message and Web site then do all the selling. You can take as much time as you need to sell your prospect. Your free recorded message can be as long as you need it to be. Your Web site can be as extensive as necessary. Once you have an email address, a postal address, and a phone number, you can take days, weeks, months even years to inform, educate, coax, and cajole your prospect automatically and robotically with the marketing system you've set up.

Your prospects will be poured into the top of your marketing funnel, which is designed to sift, sort, and categorize your prospects and customers. Your prospects (leads) will then start receiving your auto-response emails, your monthly newsletter, invitations to events, and whatever else you can think up. The possibilities are endless.

But the beauty is, once your lead enters the top of your marketing funnel, it costs you almost nothing to keep putting her through your education-based marketing program.

You are no longer limited to 60 seconds (a radio or TV ad) to make your entire sales pitch and close a sale. You are not limited by the size of a page in a newspaper or magazine. You are not limited by the space and style formats offered by the Yellow Pages. You don't need to spend $200,000 to make a long infomercial. And you are no longer limited by your meager advertising budget . . . because you no longer need a big advertising budget to do any of this kind of precision, laser-like, automated target marketing.

All you need are small, even tiny, print ads with headlines compelling enough to cause people to call your "Free 24-Hour Recorded Message Hotline," or go to your Web site, to get their free special report, Consumer Awareness Guide, or book. Radio can be a cheap advertising tool also. The "Free 24-Hour Recorded Message Hotline" is an easy message for listeners to grasp and remember with 30- and 60-second radio ads. Radio can be very cost-effective for the right products and services—those that will appeal to a broad consumer audience, not so much to a narrow, highly-targeted audience.

Radio is more of a broadcast tool, designed to reach a wide audience. Mostly, I prefer "narrow-casting" tools. I prefer to advertise exactly where my prospects (and no one else) are looking. If I want to catch fish, I go to where the fish are. And I go to where the fish are concentrated most densely. I want to go fishing in a barrel packed with fish, not the ocean. I definitely don't want to fish in the desert. Direct mail and the Internet are "narrow-casting" marketing tools. So are the Yellow Pages and classified ads because of the way they are organized. Advertising in specialty magazines designed exactly for the audience you are trying to reach is a good bet.

If you're selling guitars, try advertising in a guitar magazine with one of your "Free 24-Hour Recorded Message Hotline" ads with a headline that says something like "11 things you must know before you buy a guitar." If you are selling ammo, run the same kind of ad in one of the NRA's publications aimed at gun owners. If you offer a product aimed at seasoned citizens, the AARP's magazine would be a place to test your ad.

With these tools and strategies, you can fish where the fish are.

The point is, you can now make your ads small and cheap because you no longer need to rely on big ads in traditional media to do all your selling. You just need an ad big enough for a headline, a headline so intriguing that your readers will have to call your hotline or visit your Web site to find out the rest of the story.

One of my favorite ads was the ad for **GoDaddy.com** that ran during the Super Bowl. The ad featured an enormous-chested woman in a tight T-shirt with the phrase "GoDaddy.com" emblazoned across her chest. And that was about it. The ad did not say what the service was. But it was attention-getting.

I went immediately to my computer to find out what this company was selling. I guess everyone watching the Super Bowl did too because I couldn't get into the site. But I was certainly curious. Turns out the company provides Internet marketing tools, including domain name registration, an online Web site building tool, a merchant account service, and most tools and services needed by those of us who market on the Internet. The ad was certainly successful for GoDaddy.com.

They understood the purpose of their Super Bowl ad. It's purpose was to get me to go to their Web site, to then entice me to give them my email address by offering me free stuff. GoDaddy's plan worked on me. I'm a happy GoDaddy.com customer. That's where I store my domain names. I've bought other products from them also. GoDaddy.com understands Internet marketing.

Turn your business card into a power-packed lead generation tool

Your business card can be a powerful marketing tool.

Unfortunately, most business cards are snoresville and make no impression whatsoever. They just get tossed out or thrown in a drawer with everyone else's business card, never to see the light of day again.

You want your business card to look professional, but also turn it into a piece that your prospects will want to keep around and refer to. Include all the basic information: company name, logo, your name, phone numbers, email address, and Web site address.

Make your Web site address jump out above all else, because the Web site is today's brochure. And, because you are now a master marketer, your Web site is not like other Web sites. It's a multi-media PowerPoint presentation that dazzles your prospects.

Be sure to include the toll-free number for your "Free Recorded Message," which should also jump out. Your business card might include an ad on the back for a free special report for all who call the toll-free number to listen to the Free Recorded Message.

The point is, don't make your business card look like everyone else's card.

We don't live in the 1950s anymore. This is the 21st century. You'll be giving your business card to your very best leads, people you've actually met. Make your business card a piece people won't throw away or toss in a drawer.

For some kinds of services and businesses (carpet cleaning, plumbing, lawn care, handyman work, office products, florists, caterers, pizza delivery, other home delivery services, and many more) consider making your business card a magnet that will stick to a refrigerator.

Today you can have a business card with a chip that can contain a 30 second recorded message from you. The card includes a printed dot that says, "Press Here." The recorded message will then play. When ordered in quantity, you can have these cards made for about $1 apiece, not a whole lot more expensive than a regular business card—but one that will deliver a whole lot more bang for the marketing dollar spent.

You can also make your business card a fold-over card, a kind of mini-booklet brochure that can contain more information. What if you combined all these elements in your business card? It's a card, a fold-over, two-panel mini-brochure, a refrigerator magnet, and includes a recorded message.

Don't worry about looking hokey with such a business card. People will love it and admire you for your ingenuity and creativity. People will want to do business with someone so smart, interesting, and different. You'll see people playing with your business card, listening to the recorded message on your business card over and over again and showing it to others.

Very few people will throw away such an unusual, talking business card. Your card will be a novelty, a conversation starter. It will become the center of attention, passed around at parties.

Your business card should be a stunning attention-getter. Make your business card an important part of your overall marketing strategy that ties in with all your other marketing.

Conduct surveys to find qualified leads

Surveys are great tools to use in the right situation.

Surveys are, in fact, a great tool to use if you are in the lead generation business or if you are offering a wide range of products and services.

The purpose of the survey is simply to ask your prospect what he wants, what he's interested in—and then sell him what he's just told you he wants.

This is what politicians do.

President Clinton and his advisors were obsessed with conducting surveys and focus groups to find out what voters were thinking, what was on their minds, what they wanted. And then Clinton would craft his message exactly according to what the polls were telling him and his speechwriters.

President Clinton was a master politician. He was a master marketer and salesman. His approach was scientific. The survey data came in. He crafted his message accordingly.

We can do the same thing in all our marketing and sales work. We can conduct surveys both to find qualified prospects, and also to help us zero in more accurately on what our existing customers want.

Another great feature of surveys is that people like filling them out. People love an opportunity to give their opinions about things. You can also offer a reward to those who fill out and return your survey—perhaps a free special report on a subject you know is of interest to your reader.

A well-crafted letter and survey to a good list should be able to get a 15 percent or even a 20 percent response rate.

The answers you get back from your surveys should then be organized and entered into a database.

Let's say you are selling a variety of health products. Health care expenses account for about one-seventh of the entire U.S. economy, so the virtue of this field is that everyone is interested in their health. Everyone has concerns about health, the quality of health care, the cost of health care, and government policy on health care.

And most people will be interested in completing a survey on their health care if they believe their participation in the survey might lead to better health, lower health care costs, and a longer or healthier life. Senior citizens are especially concerned about health care. So you might start by targeting your letter to the over-60 crowd.

Here's how you might begin your letter, the goal being to persuade your reader to complete and return your survey:

National Research Survey On America's Health Care Needs and Concerns

Dear Mrs. Jones,

You have been specially selected to participate in this National Research Survey on America's Health Care Needs and Concerns.

The results of this survey will be submitted in a report to Congress and the President of the United States.

I am hoping you will take just a few minutes of your time to complete this important research poll.

Your participation will help ensure that your voice is counted and heard as the President and Congress prepare to reform Medicare and change how health care is delivered in America.

The results of this survey report will also be submitted to America's leading pharmaceutical companies and medical research institutions.

In addition, all participants in this survey will receive a free copy of the final survey report.

Your individual answers will be held in confidence. Only the overall results will be made public.

We have selected 355,000 citizens from across America to participate in this poll, representing every congressional district.

```
    Because this survey is so large, you can be
sure Congress and the White House will study the
results carefully. And it will have a major im-
pact on the Medicare and health care debate in
Congress over the coming months, when crucial
decisions on Medicare and the delivery of health
care will be made.

    So I hope you will make a special point of
completing and returning your survey for process-
ing today.
```

The survey letter starts this way because you must give your reader some compelling reasons to take the time and effort to fill out and return the survey.

The incentive in this case is the promise of having an impact on the health care and Medicare-reform debate taking place in Congress.

The incentive is having one's voice heard and counted by the powerful—important decision-makers whose decisions will have a major impact on all of our lives.

People vote in elections because they want their voice, their opinion, to count. People will fill out a survey like this for the same reason.

The letter will continue to develop these points.

The survey questions then become very important.

The survey should begin with a series of public policy issue questions concerning Medicare and health care delivery in America, questions along the lines of:

- Do you think Medicare should be changed to be a program only for those who can't afford health insurance?

- Are you in favor of more government control over health care, or less?

- Do you believe government should guarantee health care for all Americans?

- How do you rate the overall quality of health care in America?

- Are you for or against the President's proposal to . . .?

- Would you like to see Congress make all your medical and health care expenses tax-deductible?

After you complete the public policy questions, you start to move into more personal questions.

- What is your age range?

- What is your income range?

- Approximately how much do you spend on medical treatment each year?

- How much do you spend on prescription drugs each year?

- How much do you spend on vitamins each year?

- How much do you spend on supplements each year?

- Which prescription drugs do you use most?

- Do you now have health insurance?

- How concerned are you about the quality of your current coverage?

- What is your weight?

- What is your height?

- Do you belong to a gym or health club?

- How much exercise do you do a week?

- What kinds of regular exercise do you focus on?

- How do you rate your overall health?

And there are all kinds of other related questions you might ask, depending on the information you need. Can you see how the answers to such questions could be very helpful to a marketer of health products?

Your survey should be an impressive, very official-looking document, a four-page booklet at a minimum. I often construct 8-page surveys. Your survey should look like it might have been produced by a government agency—perhaps the Census Bureau, or an academic or medical research institution.

And, as you promised in your letter, you will deliver an impressive report to Congress and the White House on the results of the survey, which truly can have an impact on the policy debate.

You do everything you say you will do with the survey, including delivering a copy of the final report to all who participated.

You now have an enormous number of great leads for your health-related products. The value of these leads will then be determined by your "conversion rate"—that is, what percentage of leads become customers. It then becomes a mathematical equation how much you can spend to acquire a lead.

Of course, your "conversion rate" will be affected dramatically, up or down, by the quality of your survey questions, the products you are selling and the skill of your conversion campaign. The quicker you follow up with your conversion program, the more productive your leads.

As you can see, I'm a huge fan of the survey as a marketing tool. It's a tool I often pull out of my kit.

Chapter Twelve

How to use the Internet to automate your marketing

Turn your Web site into a PowerPoint presentation

The Web site is the brochure of the 21st century.

But unlike the old static brochure that serves little if any true marketing purpose, your Web site is an absolutely critical marketing tool. Your Web site is an integral part of your entire marketing strategy.

Most businesses treat their Web sites as an afterthought. They pay a Web site designer (usually one with no marketing background) to put up a site and that's it. The site then just sits there without ever changing—much like the old-fashioned brochure that just sat there (usually in the company's closet gathering dust).

But your Web site can be changed everyday. You can use your Web site as a bulletin board for late breaking news on new projects you are offering. All your marketing media should promote your Web site. Your Web site can be a repository for all your archived newsletters, special reports, blogs, books, audio recordings, and videos. Your Web site can be populated with compelling sales-oriented audio and video. Your Web site can be a dynamic, interactive, full-blown PowerPoint and multimedia presentation.

Your Web site, for very little cost, can make your small business look as big and powerful as the world's largest corporations. You cannot be in business in any serious way today without a terrific interactive Web site.

When people want to learn about you and your company, the first place they will go is to the Internet to check out your Web site.

If you have no Web site, or if your Web site is boring and unimpressive, people will assume your business is not real. You will be judged, in many cases, by your Web site because that's all many of your prospects have to go on. But the purpose of your Web site is not primarily image building, which is how most businesses use their Web site. They have a Web site because they know they must. But they don't know what to do with their Web site.

The power of Google AdWords

I'm having a lot of fun with this tool, an incredibly powerful engine for generating leads and testing messages and themes. And it does not require a lot of money if you proceed cautiously and correctly.

I've become a bit of a Google AdWords junky.

I'll summarize how it works. You'll have to try it for yourself and do a lot of tinkering with this tool before you begin to understand how to make it work for you.

You can waste a lot of money if you aren't careful.

So here's how it works.

People go to the Internet to find information about subjects or to find products. What they do is type "keywords" and phrases into Google on their browser. They then wait a few seconds and see what pops up in the search listing.

Google is the world's most popular search engine. Almost everyone uses Google for his or her searches. And Google powers the searches for many other lesser search engines as well, including AOL, Ask Jeeves, EarthLink, Hot Bot, and others.

What Google does is allow you to bid on keywords and phrases. The keywords you've selected and bid on are then linked by Google to mini-ads Google allows you to create (in Google's format) for display on searches of the keywords and phrases you've selected for your ads. Your ads are linked to your Web site, or the Web site you've created for the product you are selling.

There are some important tricks to making Google AdWords work.

Trick #1

Select narrow keywords and phrases that describe exactly what you are selling. If your keywords are too broad or too popular, you will spend a fortune to get your ad listed high enough in searches to have any impact.

The keyword "computers" would not be a good keyword for most of us because we would be going up against Dell, Microsoft, and the huge computer companies. And there are so many companies selling computers, especially on the Internet, that we would get lost—like a grain of sand on a beach.

What you want to use Google AdWords for is a specialized product. Suppose, just for fun, you test the keyword "Iguana."

According to Google, I can have a near monopoly on the word "Iguana" for almost nothing. And, according to Google's "Traffic Estimator" function, I will be the very first listing for about 10 cents a click for anyone looking for information on Iguanas.

Also, according to Google's "Traffic Estimator" function, there seem to be quite a lot of people searching for information on Iguanas. Why is that?

Well, I did not know this before, but it turns out the Iguana is a popular pet. More importantly, people who own an Iguana as a pet, love their Iguana, are Iguana fanatics. These Iguana owners worry about the health of their Iguana. They want a healthy Iguana so their Iguana can live a long, healthy, and happy life.

So a plausible business strategy is to craft a product, specifically designed for Iguana owners, perhaps a book titled something like: "How to Make Your Iguana a Healthy, Happy, Long-living Iguana."

Judging by the number of clicks I see estimated for the keyword "Iguana," my guess is someone could make a healthy profit producing just such a book and using Google AdWords to market it.

Google AdWords is a great tool for entrepreneurs and marketers to reach niche markets with highly targeted and specialized niche products.

Trick #2

Make sure the Web site your Google ads are linked to are precisely on point with the keywords you've bought and the subject of your ad. Do not link your ads to your general site, which might be offering many services and products. Link your ad to a Web site and response or order form specifically designed for your keyword and Google ad.

Trick #3

Test different headlines on your ad. You'll find an enormous difference in the number of clicks and inquiries generated by the various headlines you test. Google only allows very short headlines on ads, a maximum of 25 characters. So you have to really boil your message down—a great exercise for ad writers.

Trick #4

Do not become obsessed with the number of clicks your ads attract. I can always design an ad that will generate an avalanche of clicks. But that will just cost a ton of money. That's great for Google, but not for you. What counts are quality clicks. What counts is how many clicks turn into inquiries, and how many inquiries are converted into sales.

Trick #5

What Google wants are lots of clicks. What Google wants is for you to pay a high cost for each click you get on your ad and Web site. Because that's how Google makes money.

So Google will cancel your ad if it's not making enough money for Google. And Google will keep moving your ad down the listing (until it disappears, or nearly disappears) if your ad is not attracting traffic. If you pay a lot per click, and if your ad is okay, you can stay high on the Google keyword search listing.

But that's not what you want. You want to pay as little as possible per click, and have a high percentage of your clicks turn into sales. You also want enough traffic to keep Google happy, that is to keep your ad listed first, or very high up in listings for the keywords you've chosen. So your job is to select the right narrowly focused keywords and phrases, to then design ads for those keywords that will allow you to attract quality clicks—a high enough percentage of which will become customers—at as low a cost as possible. And don't forget to link your ad to a Web page that is exactly on message.

The brilliance of Google AdWords

The great feature of the Google AdWords system is that you can test ideas, words, and phrases in minutes. I can find out what's working and not working. When I'm writing a sales or marketing letter designed for print, I'll often go into Google AdWords to experiment with different headlines, phrases, and keywords—just to see what pulls best.

But the best way to learn how to use Google AdWords successfully is to go there and just start playing with it. You will make mistakes. You will waste some money, as I certainly did and continue to do with all my experimenting. But it will be money well spent, because you will learn a lot about marketing and human psychology by how people respond to your ads on Google.

Google AdWords is like a stern teacher that slaps my wrist with a ruler every time I break the laws of marketing. The system forces me to tailor my product, my service to the market, not to try to mold the market to fit my product. It forces me to sell people what they are asking me for with their keyword searches and clicks.

That's why I'm such a Google AdWords junky.

Yahoo has a similar tool called Overture. But I have not found it as productive as Google AdWords. What an awesome company Google is!

I just hope Google does not ruin AdWords by becoming too greedy and raising its cost-per-click minimum bids.

How to use your Web site

Your Web site and your entire Internet marketing strategy should be about collecting email addresses and other information on qualified prospects (leads). Though your Web site serves a PR and image-building purpose by making you look bigger than you are, that's not its primary purpose.

Its primary purpose is to act like a magnet that will attract qualified leads who are surfing the Internet. How do you do this?

You do this primarily by putting bait out there on the Internet, bait that gets the fish you're looking for to bite (leads). The bait I use are free reports, free books, free video and audio on subjects that are exactly in line with what I am selling. Sometimes I only ask for an email address and a name in exchange for the free report or free downloadable book I am offering. What I'm after is a way (an email address) to contact my lead so I can feed my lead more free bait (information) on the subject I now know she's interested in.

I will use Google AdWords and Overture to place my ads on the Internet offering the free book or free report. In addition, I will rely on great search engine optimization of my site that ensures I appear on the first page of searches conducted of the "keywords" and phrases I have selected to promote my site and landing pages. More on this crucial marketing tool in a minute. And I will place banner ads on Web sites that are on the subject I am promoting.

I don't like to pay cash for banner ads. I always try to negotiate a pay-per order deal. I might offer 50 cents for a lead and 50 or 75 percent of the income from a cash order, for example, because what I'm really after is the name (the lead), not the money yet. I don't like to part with cash when running banner ads unless I know a site has a great track-record of producing results.

After I capture the email address, I run the lead through my program of free newsletters and emails that are full of valuable information. The program I develop for each lead I collect is designed to build trust so that this prospect shares more information with me. I then come to a point when I offer the lead something to buy—perhaps an invitation to a seminar or workshop on the subject I know she's interested in. The seminar could be in a conference room at a physical location, or it could be a tele-seminar or a webinar. Teleseminars are conducted via a conference phone call, with many people on the line. A webinar is a live seminar conducted on the Internet. You can have teleseminars and webinars for both your prospects and existing customers.

The teleseminar and webinar are tremendous marketing tools. As with all marketing, the key to ensuring attendance at your teleseminars and webinars (or physical seminars for that matter) is to make sure you are on a subject that is of intense interest to your prospects and customers—in other words, exactly in line with the message that brought your prospect in the door in the first place.

Your Web site should have an archive of all your past teleseminars and webinars that can be accessed again on an ongoing basis, often for a fee.

And as with all marketing, the key to success is for the product you delivered with your free offer ad to vastly exceed your prospect's expectations. The product you deliver, even your free products, must exceed your prospect's expectations by such a wide margin that your prospect will wonder how you could ever top the free item with a product your prospect must pay for.

If you always exceed expectations, you will have no trouble making the next sale.

As with all your marketing, the goal must be sales—then transforming first-time buyers into ongoing relationships that lead to more and bigger sales.

You bring your leads in with free offers, but you have a series of upgrades in mind that can go on almost forever.

American Express does this as well or better than any company.

American Express sells primarily prestige, status, and exclusivity. American Express has the regular green card, then the Gold Card, the Platinum Card, and finally the Centurion Card (also known as the "Black Card"). The annual membership fee for Black Card holders is $2,500.

Whether you use the desire of prestige, status, and exclusivity as your primary motivator, or some other motivator to induce a desire in your customers to start moving up your ladder and buy more, the point is, you must have a ladder.

The first rung is for your prospect to give you her name and email address in exchange for something of value that's free. After you've run your prospects through a program of giving them more free valuable stuff, you want them to move up to the next rung on your ladder, which is to buy something from you, something relatively inexpensive. But eventually, just like American Express, you will want to find out who your Gold, Platinum, and Black Card customers are.

This is the process of sifting, sorting, and segmentation that must be the purpose of your marketing system.

What's great about the Internet is that almost all of it can be done automatically and robotically—as well as very cheaply—with technology, once you have the programs and systems set up, and once you have found through trial and error (testing) a winning offer and formula.

Building your own Web site is easy . . . even for me

There's no need to hire a techie to build your Web site or hire a web-master to maintain it.

You can do it yourself if you just work on it for a weekend. And then you will have a new skill that will serve you for the rest of your life.

I'm not a techie and I built my own Web site by using a super-easy online Web site building tool called **CityMax.com**. Another good one is **SiteBuildIt.com**. You can also find an online Web site building tool at GoDaddy.com. There are many others as well. Microsoft's FrontPage is also fairly easy to learn. FrontPage is a program you install on your computer. But the easiest thing is just to use one of the good online site builder programs.

I couldn't believe how easy it was. And every Internet marketing tool you need is on the Internet, ready for downloading (if it's not already included in the online site builder's package). And sellers of these products are experts at walking technological idiots like me step-by-step through the process and teaching me how to do everything. I don't know programming. I just grab the off-the-shelf technology and use it.

You can grab: auto-response email programs that automatically follow-up with your prospects and customers; automatic newsletter sequential broadcast programs; flash pages already set up and ready to go with your company name and logo; easy-to-use programs to design your own pop-up ads; programs to upload video to your site; shopping cart and online credit card processing systems; and broadcast voice and video programs where you can send out emails that include a message with your voice.

There's no limit to what you can do with your site today to transform it into a PowerPoint, multi-media presentation that reaches out across cyberspace and robotically snags your hottest prospects—all while you're playing golf or sleeping at night. And you can do it on your own with absolutely no knowledge of programming. You don't really need to know technology at all. You just need to know marketing and what tools are available today to make your marketing easy and automatic. You can then either learn how to use the tools yourself, or higher a modern handyman (a techie) to help you use them. I think it's fun to learn how to use these tools myself.

Just as the typewriter before 1980 was an essential tool everyone had to learn in school, the computer and the Internet are the modern communications and marketing tools everyone in business must have an understanding of in order to make life as easy, stress-free, and enjoyable.

Everyday, more and more sales are being transacted on line. This year (2006) more than $60 BILLION in services and merchandise will be sold on the Internet. If you are not fluent with this marketing media, you and your business will be left behind. I'm learning new things everyday about Internet marketing, and I'm having tons of fun doing it.

Automatic email marketing

Email is your primary communications tool on the Internet. Without email, your Web site is just like the old-fashioned brochure. It just sits there looking pretty, but does nothing for your business.

Auto-response emails

One of the most powerful email marketing tools is the auto-responder.

This is a series of emails that you write and set up in advance. This series of emails is sent to your prospects and customers in a pre-set sequence. For example, if someone orders your free special report, they would immediately be sent the special report and begin receiving a series of emails, perhaps every other day on the subject you know they are interested in—which is the subject of the special report they ordered.

For those who order my free special report, I have up to one year's worth of emails written for them in a queue, ready to be sent to them on the assigned day. The assigned day is based on the day of the order, so they would receive an immediate email in response to their order. The next emails would be sent on day 2, day 4, day 6, etc. The emails are short, but always contain useful and valuable information on the subject my prospect is interested in.

This is how you stay a welcome guest and don't become an annoying pest.

You want your prospects to look forward to the arrival of your email. You might have a title for your auto-response email series. A series I send is titled "Ben's Secrets to Successful Direct Marketing." Each email contains a valuable tip for direct marketers and people interested in direct marketing. No one ever unsubscribes to this online newsletter (auto-response email series) because everyone on this auto-response list finds the emails valuable and useful. Some have asked, "Have you ever thought of simply publishing your emails as a book?" The truth is, most of my auto-response email communications are pulled directly from books, articles, and special reports I've already written. I'm just recycling the material in a different format.

Every now and then, you give your auto-response email list an opportunity to buy something from you. Once someone buys something for the first time, they are immediately entered into a new auto-response series of email messages geared toward first-time buyers.

When they buy a second time from you, they are entered into yet another auto-response email program, with messages geared toward those who you know are more committed, more loyal. This is how you move your prospects and customers up your buying ladder. And it's all done automatically, with a preset series of email messages scheduled to go out in sequence (every other day, starting with the date of the first inquiry or order). Once the name is in your system, it's all automatic and robotic from then on. You don't have to do too much, except check it every now and then.

The auto-response email system also creates your list for you, because as soon as someone fills out an order form to receive your free special report, this information is automatically entered into a database list of other names who are getting the same series of pre-scheduled emails.

Your auto-response email system and computer do all your sorting and sifting of prospects and customers for you. This is how you leverage your time. Your computer is now your sales force.

You can then spend your time creating great product and providing great service (or playing golf and spending time with your kids) instead of pounding the pavement making cold calls.

I will repeat this point again, because it's so important. So please pay attention.

Ninety percent of your communications should be educational and informative. Only 10 percent should aim for a sale. If you stay true to this ratio, you will always be a welcome guest in the homes of your prospects and customers. And you can now afford to do this because email is so cheap. You can afford to be patient.

The company I use for my auto-response email program is **Intellicontactpro.com.** Another good system is offered by **Aweber.com.**

There are others as well. But either of these companies will take you where you want to go. You just enroll in their program for about $29 or $39 a month and your auto-response email program is ready to roll.

You can also buy auto-response email programs that you install in your computer. I prefer just to pay the $29 or $39 a month and have another company do the technical work. I just write the auto-response email messages, put them in the order I want my prospects and customers to receive them, and they go out when they are supposed to. If there's a glitch, I call the company and let them know. They check it out and fix the glitch if there is one, or they tell me what I did wrong.

I'm a marketer. I mostly want to spend my time creating the message (and messages), and scheduling when my customers and prospects receive my messages. I don't want to spend time fixing technical glitches. I want to use the tools, but I don't want to be a full-time mechanic. That's why I like the online Web site builder programs, the online auto-response email programs, the online shopping cart and credit card processing programs, the online pop-up ad generator programs and the online video and audio generator programs.

These online programs allow you to have experts and engineers do what they do best (the techie stuff), so you can focus on what you do best (your business and marketing). And this is very important: Using these online resources allows you to do enough of the Web site and Internet marketing yourself without your company ever being held hostage by a disgruntled computer or webmaster guy. There's no reason to be intimidated by technology anymore. All you need is available in idiot-proof, off-the-shelf online programs that even a technological illiterate like me can use with ease.

The auto-response email programs are especially easy to use. Auto-response email is an essential tool for creating your hands-free, automatic marketing system.

As with all gadgets, the best way to learn how to use it is just to spend a day or so fiddling with it. I still can't figure out how to program my VCR, but I can build my Web site and assemble an auto-response email program for my prospects and customers with ease.

How to rank high on search engines

We've discussed pay-per-click advertising (Google AdWords and Overture) and running banner ads to drive traffic to your Web site and landing pages. These paid forms of advertising are the quickest way to drive traffic to your Web site.

The free and permanent method is to make sure your Web site is ranked high on the major search engines for the keywords and phrases people type into search engines when looking for the kind of product or service you are offering. Really, the only search engines to focus on are Google and Yahoo, because 90 percent of the searches are done with these search engines, or by search engines that are powered either by Google or Yahoo.

Your goal is to be on the first page of "search results" when the keywords and phrases that best describe your product are typed in by Web surfers. People rarely look deeper than the second page of search results.

So here are the big keys to making sure your Web site ranks high on searches your most likely future customers are conducting right now:

Key #1:
Select the right keywords and phrases.

You must focus on selecting the "best keywords and phrases" for your site that describe your product. And they should be as focused as possible. If you are a store that sells computers, the best keyword for you is not "computers." Sure, you should include it on your list because that's what you do. But better would be "Great Falls computers" and "computers Great Falls." That way you will get people from your area looking at your site, the folks who are most likely to come into your store. You should include the names of surrounding towns as well.

The right keywords and phrases are not always the ones you expect. There are many keyword-tracking tools on the Web designed to help you find the best keywords and phrases. Overture has a good one called the Overture Keyword Selector Tool. You can find it at:

http://inventory.overture.com/d/searchinventory/suggestion/.
Another good one can be found at: **www.trafficology.com/research/.**
To find the best keywords and phrases, you must:

1) Get into the heads of your likely customers. Imagine what keywords you would be typing into search engines if you were looking for your product.

2) Test your keyword clicks and conversions by using a small campaign on Google AdWords.

This process will help you identify the best keywords and phrases to maximize traffic to your site. You will need at least 30 of the best keywords and phrases that relate to your product or service. Think of every possible combination your prospects might type into a search engine. Be sure you include keywords that are as specific to you as possible, as well as the broad categories that describe your business.

Just remember that if you are a small computer store in Great Falls, you will not rank high for general searches of just the word "computers." Those spots are taken by the big boys, Microsoft, Dell, etc. You will certainly want to include the word "computers" because that's your business. But you must also have keywords that specifically describe you and not Dell or Microsoft. You want to be #1 for those who type in "Great Falls computers" or "computers Great Falls."

Key #2:
Get your site linked by other sites that are listed in search engines.

Search engines find sites by crawling through the Web from link to link with programs called "spiders." So having other sites linked to yours is critical. Search engines also track "link popularity." If lots of people are clicking links to your site, this helps your ranking. In fact, once you are listed, the search engines then track how many people are clicking onto your site. This dramatically affects your ranking for the keywords you've selected.

There are several good ways to have your site linked by other sites. The simplest way is to ask. That is, ask a site you want your link to appear on to link you. Offer to provide a link on your site to their site in exchange. Many will say yes because they know links help them.

You can also find out who is linking to your competitors by using a linking tool such as **Zeus**, **Arelis,** or **Link Spider**. If you enter the URL of your competitor, the program will give you a list of all pages that link to your competitor. These programs then allow you to email these sites, or you can contact them directly by phone to ask for a link to your site or to propose a link exchange.

There may be directories of companies in your industry. Be sure your site is included in these directories with your link.

Run ad campaigns on Google AdWords. You'll be amazed at how many sites will include your ad as part of the Google AdSense program. That's where people earn income by running Google's pay-per-click ads. These can count as links to sites.

Key #3:
Put the most important keywords on every page of your site.

Search engines want to make sure the keywords and content of your site are clearly connected. If the search engine is not finding your keywords in the text of your site, this hurts, often fatally. Have your keywords scattered throughout your pages, but only where they make sense. Search engines consider excess repeating of keywords spamming or "stuffing." You might put your keywords in bold in a couple of places. I'm told that can help, but I'm not sure about that.

Key #4:
Use the <h1> and <h2> tags and put your keywords between them.

This is just some HTML code you should be aware of. With the online and off-the-shelf Web site building programs that make it easy for the layman to build a site, it's not necessary to know any HTML code anymore. But it's useful to know some. All the good Web site building programs allow you to edit using code or in a Word-style program that acts exactly like a word processor. But you should become familiar with some basic HTML code to optimize your site.

Key #5:
Include your keywords in the ALT attribute of your IMG tag.

This is some more basic code you should become familiar with.

Key #6:
Include your keywords in the TITLE attribute of your <A> tag.

Ditto. More HTML code you should know to optimize your search engine ranking. It's not so tough to learn, and it's kind of fun.

Key #7:
Have a title for each page that includes your most important keywords.

Search engines want relevant titles of Web pages listed on their searches. A title with the main keywords tells search engines and readers that this Web site is on point and on message.

Key #8:
Have a unique title for every page.

Otherwise the search engines will think you are spamming them or that the material is repetitive. You want every page of your Web site to come across as unique and interesting in the eyes of the search engine, but also on point with the keywords and phrases being searched.

Key #9:
Make your title one that describes benefits to the reader.

Search engines reward you with higher rankings when lots of people click through to your site. Think of your title for each page as your headline in all your ad copy. But don't use empty "hype" words like "greatest" and "best ever." Both search engines and readers discard such empty hype. Make your titles compellingly factual and on message.

Key #10:
Include your keywords at the very top and very bottom of every page in your site.

But do so in a way that makes sense, not in a way that the search engines will think is spamming.

Key #11:
Don't use too much java script or flash programming.

Search engines don't like lots of code. Search engines like clean sites with a minimum of code.

Key #12:
Include your physical address on your Web site.

You will probably want to include the city you're in as among your keywords anyway. So you should include your physical address in the text of your site everywhere that it makes sense to do so. I don't know for sure, but I have a sense that search engines like sites with physical addresses.

Key #13:
Submit your site to search engines.

This is easy. There's no need to hire a company to submit your site for you, but you can if you want. Each search engine shows you how. Follow their instructions very carefully. Here's an important tip. Include the true and complete URL for your Web site homepage, not another page that is forwarded to your home page.

The big search engines show you how to submit your site. Submit your site to Google by going here:

http://www.google.com/addurl/?continue=/addurl.

Submit your site to Yahoo by going here:
https://login.yahoo.com/config/login?.src=srch&.done=http://submit.sea rch.yahoo.com/free/request.

Just by doing this, you'll end up on the two search engines that handle or power about 90 percent of all searches. But it's just as easy to submit your site to the other search engines as well. In addition to Google and Yahoo, here are the other major search engines to submit your site to:

- Overture
- Inktomi
- MSN
- AskJeeves
- Open Directory Project
- LookSmart
- Lycos
- AlltheWeb
- AltaVista

There are hundreds of others. But this will do it for you.

Key #14:
Have a clean, simple site.

As you are building, editing, and changing your site, a lot of excess code is often left sitting there not doing anything. The site appears to work fine because the excess code is not visible and is not performing any function. Clean it up. Streamline your HTML and other coding. Search engines are interested in sites that provide lots of good information. This is what makes the search engines valuable.

Key #15:
Run pay-per-click ad campaigns on Google AdWords and Overture.

This will get traffic running through your Web site, a key factor for your search engine rankings. And it will speed up the linking process with other sites in your field.

Key #16:
Have your site checked out by a Web site search engine optimization expert.

I have very limited knowledge of code myself. Every couple of months I'll have a Web site search engine optimization expert check out my site and eliminate any problems search engines might have with my site. Consider this like taking your car in to have a tune up. It's cheap and well worth it.

Key #17:
Never try to fool the search engines.

The search engines want to list sites that are truly valuable. They don't want a lot of junk coming up when surfers conduct searches. They want legitimate companies, legitimate services, and legitimate people to come up in searches. The search engines are on a relentless quest to crush and stamp out spammers and scammers. And the search engines are a lot smarter at this than you and I are. The search engines keep their criteria for listing and ranking sites a secret, and they change their criteria all the time, precisely to make it very difficult to fool them.

So never try to trick search engines into listing you or ranking you high. That's about the surest way I know to make sure you are locked out of a search engine. For example, don't repeat your keywords over and over again in the text of your Web site. This is considered spamming the search engine. Use your keywords in your text and marketing copy in a way that makes sense, as you would if you were not concerned about the search engines. Don't try to hide keywords in images or other locations. Don't keep submitting your site to search engines repeatedly. That's considered spamming also. Submit your site to the search engines and wait a couple of months. If your site is still not listed, call the search engine and see if there is something you can do. Probably not. Just wait, be patient. Or consult with your search engine optimization expert. But if you've followed the steps I've outlined here, your site will be listed and should rank high for the searches of your target audience.

How do I find out if my site is listed on a search engine?

There are several ways. One is to go to the search engine (not your browser) and type in the full URL of your site. Your site will then either come up or a message will pop up telling you your site is not listed. Another way is to type in your most focused and specific keyword or phrase (i.e., your company name) and see if your site comes up on the listing.

The bottom line

The most important factor determining the success of the online portion of your business is your success at attracting a steady stream of traffic to your Web site and landing pages. Getting listed and ranking high on search engines is not an accident. Web site "Trafficology" is a science like all other areas of marketing.

Here's a great resource you should check out for more on this subject. Go to **www.onlinetrafficnow.com** and you will find hundreds of tips, methods, and systems for generating a massive amount of Web traffic for your site and landing pages almost immediately.

Remember, "location, location, location" are the three major words determining the value of your physical property. Search engine ranking for your keywords and phrases is the real estate of the Web.

Be sure your Web site is ready to do business

Just having a Web site is not enough. Make sure your Web site is set up to take orders and capture email addresses.

Customers are becoming comfortable with doing business online. Customers expect a real business to be able to transact business online today. Many want the convenience of being able to shop on their terms, whenever they want, from the comfort of their homes, 24/7.

Businesses that can't transact sales from their Web site have many excuses. It's a hassle. I don't know how. Lack of time. But today's technology makes it so easy, cheap, and quick. Shopping carts, security certificates, and payment options have all been taken care of for you.

Even if you still conduct 99 percent of your business offline, you look amateur if you can't conduct business online. The truth is, you'll probably be out of business in a few years if you ignore the Web as a place to market and transact your business.

Here's what you must do:

1) **Get the software.** Some Web site building systems come with shopping carts built in. If your site lacks this feature, you must buy software to set up an online shopping cart, as well as order forms, payment systems, third-party credit card processing, etc. Make sure you have all the software necessary at hand before you set up your store. If you've used a Web designer, she'll take care of all the software and form set-up for you.

2) **Pick the products you want to sell online.** You can sell just about any kind of product or service from your Web site.

3) **Set up your online product catalog if you are selling a variety of products.** The more information you provide, the better your chances of making a sale. Show photos of your products, and write detailed descriptions (bullets are effective when listing benefits). Be sure to include the price for each product!

4) **Set up your payment options.** Marketers know that the more ways your customers can pay online, the less shopping cart abandonment you'll suffer. For example, if you accept PayPal, credit cards, fax in payment, and checks, you'll convert far more sales than if you operate on a checks-only basis or if you only accept certain credit cards.

5) **Make sure you're ready to ship, fulfill, or do whatever it is you promise.** You haven't completed your sale until you can get the product to your customer's door. UPS and FedEx are very happy to help you with your shipping.

Chapter Thirteen

How to use voice and video to inject rocket fuel into your marketing

You can now add your voice to much of your marketing.

A printed page is silent. It's more effort for people to read what you have to say. But what if you could stand in the living rooms of thousands of people at once and deliver your sales presentation?

Now you can by adding audio to your Web site and by sending audio emails to your leads and customers.

And it's incredibly easy and powerful.

Most people would rather attend a seminar than read a book.

Now you can give your prospects the option of reading or hearing what you have to say.

Many, if not most, will choose hearing what you have to say.

I've already touched on this in the chapter on the power of the "24-Hour Free Recorded Message Hotline." But the same principle applies here.

When someone hears you speak, they feel they know more about you. Wouldn't you rather listen to an author read her work? I would love to listen to Ernest Hemmingway read his novels and short stories. Rather than read his poems on my own, I would rather hear Robert Frost speak his poetry. I feel I would have a better understanding of what these great writers were saying. I would have a sense from the inflections and tones in their voices what these writers want me to feel. With voice, it's easier to emphasize and draw attention to your key points. It's easier to guide your listener through your story or presentation.

A voice is just more attention-getting than text.

I'm using a Web-based service called **audiogenerator.com** to add voice to my Internet marketing.

There are other similar services out there as well. But AudioGenerator.com works well for me because it's easy to use. I don't have to do any technical stuff. I just speak my message into the phone. The recording is stored at AudioGenerator.com. A few seconds later I receive a string of code. I then insert this code on the page and in the exact spot on my site I want my audio to appear. You have a 30-minute time limit for your audio messages and presentations, which should certainly be enough.

With this tool, visitors to your site can now press a button on your home page and hear a welcome message, which should include a voice-guided description of what your listeners can find on your site. If your site includes a sales letter, you can now offer visitors the option of hearing your voice deliver the sales presentation. You can put your email communications on super-steroids by giving your readers the choice of hearing you speak your emails.

In addition, you can use voice broadcasting to leave messages on the voice mail and answering machines of your prospects and customers. With voice broadcasts you can let your prospects and customers know about a special offer, invite them to an event or share with them some valuable information they will be interested in.

Be sure to capture audio versions of your testimonials. Video as well.

The point is, adding your voice will make your marketing come alive for your prospects and customers. Instead of a flat written presentation, your marketing will become more three-dimensional, more like a real person standing in each person's living room talking. Your prospects will feel closer to you, like they have a relationship.

Adding voice to your marketing can boost your marketing returns 50 percent or more.

Add video to your Internet marketing

With video you can now put your own infomercials on your Web site. Not only can your prospects and customers hear you speak, they can see you. Some demonstrations can only be done visually. Often a picture (a video) is worth a thousand words.

Or you might want to show a conference where a number of people are speaking. It's difficult to keep track of who's talking with just audio. Very often you want to see the participants so you can connect a voice to a face.

Not only can you have video on your Web site, you can send video emails and talk to your customers face-to-face.

This was not as possible when most people had low-speed dial-up connections. But today more and more people have high-speed broadband connections that play video instantly and as well as your TV set. Imagine a personalized video email going out to former customers who have not bought from you in a while where you tell them, "I miss you. In fact I miss you so much I'll give you a _____ as my free gift if you just come into our store this week and say hello."

Streaming video on your Web site, webcasts, webinars and video email are exploding right now. And it's just as easy to incorporate into your marketing mix as audio. World class marketers understand that people learn and are moved by reading, by hearing, and by seeing. You must use all the senses to communicate your message. You must come at your prospect and customers from every angle and direction.

With print, audio, and video, your Web site and your entire Internet marketing operation can now be a traveling, talking, showing salesman who never gets tired and will work for you 24/7 without pay, even while you sleep.

You can learn more about how to inject video into your Web site and email messaging by going to **talkway.com** or **instantvideogenerator.com**

Chapter Fourteen
The power of electronic seminars

You can now have a video conference on the Web (webinars) or an audio conference on the phone (teleconferences or teleseminars). This was impossible for the little guy a few years ago, but now anyone can afford this powerful marketing tool.

These tools mean you no longer need to pay for an expensive conference room at a hotel. Nor will the participants need to travel long distances. Everyone can participate from the comfort of his or her office or home. A conference can include a few people or thousands of people. These electronically conducted conferences or seminars can be used to:

1) Introduce a new product
2) Share information
3) Build relationships with your prospects and customers
4) Reward your best customers by giving them a way to participate as an "insider"

As with all marketing you can have electronic conferences for various levels; for example, one for your "Silver Members," another for your "Gold Members," and another for your "Platinum Members." Your reasons for holding an electronic conference or seminar are limited only by your imagination. Some are free. Some you charge for. It all depends on what you are trying to achieve.

Is it a schmoozing event where you share some valuable information for free? Is the purpose to sell a product? Or is the electronic seminar itself the product—for example, part of a very expensive Coaching Program for Business Executives featuring Michael Dell and Bill Gates as speakers? Now that's something a lot of people would pay big money for!

Or it could be more modest. I've seen teleseminars and webinars sold for $1, $10, $30, $100, and $1,000. Whether you charge or not, and what you charge, depends entirely on what your purpose is and who the audience is—which is no different than all your other marketing efforts.

The same principles apply in all marketing. Just the tools change. The webinar, Web conference, teleconference, and teleseminar are just some of the newest and most potent arrows in the marketer's quiver that fit perfectly with the sell-by-educating-and-informing philosophy described and advocated throughout this book.

The electronic conference can be conducted in a way that everyone participates, or you can have just a few designated participants where everyone else is muted and can only listen. You'll have to have designated speakers if you have hundreds or thousands of participants in the conference or seminar.

You should not start off with a large electronic conference at first. Start small with just a few people and get used to this medium. As with any performance, you need to rehearse your act before you hit the big stage.

When you promote your electronic conference, you'll do it exactly as you do all your marketing.

1) You'll want an attention-getting headline for your electronic conference (i.e., "Nine ways to double the profitability of your business this year").

2) You'll need to tell people when it is, how long it will be, and how to access the conference.

3) You'll want to emphasize that this is a "By invitation only" conference.

4) You'll need to publicize the benefits participants will gain from the conference (i.e., "You'll learn how to automate your marketing so you will never need to make a sales call again").

5) If your conference is selling something, you'll want to offer an incentive for people to hear the entire presentation (i.e., "You'll want to stay on this call for the entire 60 minutes, because at

the end we'll show you how to download your free book, *How to Write Advertisements that Sell"*).

6) When you begin the conference or seminar, and if you have a large group, you will need to mute participants on the line. And you will need to explain why not everyone will be able to speak by saying something like, "Because we have a sold-out seminar today with 85 participants, we are muting the line for everyone except the featured speakers in order to cut down on background noise so everyone can hear clearly, and because we have a lot of great material to cover in a short period of time. We know how busy all of you are, so let's get started. If you have questions or comments, please just email them to _____. We'll try to answer your questions as we go and as time allows."

7) As you would with a regular conference in a physical conference room, you will want to introduce yourself and the speakers. And you will want to encourage all participants to take notes.

8) You will likely want to close out your conference with a call to action of some kind. If you were selling something, you would make the same kind of pitch you would in a marketing letter. You would give your listeners:

- Benefits to the buyer
- The offer
- Proof of your claims (i.e., testimonials, case studies, track record)
- A super-charged guarantee
- A way to order
- Incentive to order now

9) You then close out the conference by thanking everyone for participating and give everyone a way to get their free book (or other incentive reward) for staying on the call for the full

60 minutes. If necessary, you apologize for not being able to cover every question emailed in, but promise to answer all emails after the conference.

The benefits of incorporating audio and video conferencing into your marketing plan are enormous.

Here are just a few:

- o **Your reach is now global, just like the world's biggest corporations.** I still prefer teleconferences and teleseminars to the video version on the Web because not everyone has a high-speed Internet connection, but everyone has a phone. And people can participate even while driving in a car. It's also possible to offer participants a choice of participating on the Web or by phone.

- o **Increases your visibility and credibility with your clients and prospects.** You will be perceived as a market leader and highly professional. Those who conduct seminars are perceived as experts.

- o **Cements a relationship with your customers.** The more your customers see and hear you, the more loyal to you they will be. If your presentation is compelling, if the information you are sharing is valuable, you will develop a committed loyal following.

- o **It's cheap.** You no longer need to travel to meet with your customers. You no longer need to rent a conference room. Everyone can participate from wherever they happen to be.

- o **Minimal logistics.** Conducting such an electronic conference requires far less logistics and complexity than a physical seminar at a location. No hotel and travel reservations. No need to serve food, refreshments, and coffee. No name tags.

o **Replay it over and over.** You can upload the conference or seminar onto your Web site for repeat playing. If you are in the seminar or information sharing business, you can charge a fee to give your customers access to an archived library of seminars.

Here are some uses for the electronic conference or seminar:

- share valuable information that is of interest to your market;
- introduce a new product;
- conduct a class or seminar;
- showcase a book you've written;
- train salespeople and company personnel if they are dispersed geographically;
- conduct Q&A sessions with your customers and clients; and
- conduct a focus group to pilot test your marketing message.

Chapter Fifteen

Your monthly newsletter is the next best thing to printing money in your basement

Your monthly newsletter is your most powerful marketing tool for your existing customers and leads. In fact, your monthly newsletter is the closest thing to printing money in your basement. Here's why:

1) It's cheap.

2) It provides valuable information for your customers.

3) It keeps your name in front of your customers, your qualified leads, and your former customers.

I prefer postal mail rather than email as the vehicle for delivering a monthly newsletter. Postal mail has more impact than email. And a printed physical newsletter has greater perceived value than email. Email can be deleted with a keystroke. Email is a great marketing tool, but it's not the right vehicle for delivering your monthly newsletter.

Why monthly?

Because testing shows that newsletters lose their impact when they arrive less than monthly. If it's only mailed, say, quarterly, your customers will lose sight of you. In all your marketing you must be in front of your customers and prospects repeatedly and continuously. Not with heavy-handed sales pitches, but with valuable information your customers will eagerly anticipate receiving from you. When you are out of sight, you're out of mind.

More frequent newsletters certainly won't hurt you if you have enough to say. But a monthly newsletter arriving via postal mail is adequate, because you will also be communicating with your customers in other ways—for example with email, personal letters, thank you notes, perhaps thank you gifts, and holiday cards.

Here's why your monthly newsletter is the nearest thing to printing money in your basement.

Expect a $20 to $1 or even a $50 to $1 return on your investment. Let's go over the math.

Your newsletter will cost about $.80 to print and mail, including postage, or about $10 per year to send a customer your monthly newsletter. You can probably do it for 60 cents each, but the illustration is easiest to follow if we say it costs you $10 per customer per year to send your monthly newsletter.

If the profit on your average sale is $100, you would only have to make one sale to a customer every 10 years to break even on your newsletter. But what if the profit on your average sale is $300 or $1,000? If you're a lawyer, a plastic surgeon, a CPA, or you're selling office supplies or printing to businesses, your profit per sale could easily be thousands of dollars.

Maybe you're a restaurant, a dry cleaner or a hair salon, where your profit per sale is only $20. But if you can get your customer to come in once a month, that's $240 in profit per year from one customer for a marketing cost of $10.

Can you see why a monthly newsletter to your customers, prospects, and former customers is like having an ATM machine with an unlimited source of cash that you can take out any time?

So what should be in your monthly newsletter?

As with all your marketing, you should be marketing by educating and informing.

Remember, there are no boring subjects, just boring writers.

Consider what the great ad writer Claude Hopkins did for Schlitz Beer. He made Schlitz the #1 selling beer by simply describing the Schlitz process of brewing beer. He turned the brewing process into a fascinating story. I'll tell you this great story later, in Chapter 17 of this book.

You could take exactly this approach with almost any product or service. Adopt the Claude Hopkins formula for writing all your marketing materials.

Fill your newsletters with ways to respond and calls for immediate action

Your newsletter should include more than just great information.

It should also be filled with calls to action, reasons for your customers to respond. Your newsletter should always contain a special offer that expires on a date. For example, a two-for-one sale, or 30% off, or "Your haircut is free if you bring a friend with you who has never been here before"—all the usual incentives we've been talking about throughout this book to get people to buy now rather than later.

Drive your readers to your Web site. Ask them to complete and return a survey. Invite them to a special event. Inspire them to call your Free Recorded Message Hotline. Give away something free to those who call you or drop by your store.

Nothing fancy

And your newsletter should not be fancy.

Four pages (an 11" x 17" sheet folded in half, booklet style) with articles written in courier type is fine. For some reason, newsletters that are printed in courier type outperform newsletters in a Times-Roman or other desktop publishing font. What makes a newsletter different from a magazine is that it looks more timely. It looks like you rushed it out the door as soon as it came off your typewriter because the information is so hot and can't wait.

So don't spend money on fancy layouts for your newsletter. You can include a photo or two in your newsletter if you think this enhances your message. But photos are usually not necessary. You might include a photo of yourself in the regular masthead to add a personal touch to your newsletter. This is effective if you are a small-business owner or sole proprietor. People want to do business with people, not corporations.

According to the great marketer Dan Kennedy, you will lose 10 percent of your customers for every month they don't hear from you. People will simply forget who you are.

I have sometimes forgotten the name of the company I did business with that did a great job for me. I simply could not find them again. They lost contact with me.

Don't assume that, just because you sold something to someone they will remember who you are. People buy on impulse. People buy because it's convenient, because you were there when they needed your service or product. You were there at the right time. But once you're out of sight, you're out of mind.

Not sending a monthly newsletter to your customers is like flushing money down the toilet.

Chapter Sixteen
Three essential rules of marketing

Rule #1
Frequent contact is essential.

I think the question I'm asked most often is this: "Won't my customers get sick of me if I keep contacting them all the time—with my monthly newsletter, with email, with direct mail, with thank yous, with free gifts, with holiday cards?"

My answer? An emphatic "NO! Not if what you have to say is interesting and of interest to your customer." People never get sick of learning something new. This is marketing by educating.

The need for frequent regular contact is also marketing 101.

It's absolutely essential.

Does Nike stop running ads because we've already seen a Nike ad this month?

No. Nike pounds our brain relentlessly, every day. So do all the big consumer brands—Coca-Cola, McDonald's, Dell.

Professional marketers know that you must see an ad at least 20 times before it makes any impression on your brain. We know that it's hard work to carve out a niche in someone's brain. McDonald's knows that the minute it pulls its ads off the air, fewer people come into their restaurants. If McDonald's stopped advertising for a year and if Burger King advertised like McDonald's, McDonald's would lose much of its market share to Burger King.

It's hard to imagine, but McDonald's would pretty well disappear as a brand in people's minds if it were to stop advertising. Howard Johnson's was the McDonald's of its day in the 1950s and 1960s. Everyone used to go to Howard Johnson's for a burger and a shake. And, frankly, the food and shakes were a whole lot better than McDonald's. But McDonald's is a marketing machine. So Howard Johnson's fell off the pace.

Relentless, mind-pounding repetition is the key to effective market-ing. Don't assume your customers know who you are just because they received a mailing or bought from you once.

But your marketing must always be interesting to grab and hold the attention of your audience. That's where your brainpower must comes in.

Rule #2
If it's working, keep doing it. Keep firing.

With all your marketing you'll be testing and tracking your results.

You'll be testing sources, lists, advertising media, headlines, offers, benefits, and other aspects of your message along with graphics and packaging.

So here's the key.

When you find something that's working for you, keeping doing it over and over again.

I'm amazed at how many people just mail once, even if the mailing is an astonishing success. If your special report, your Consumer Protection Guide, your newsletter, your postcard, your direct mail letter, or your di-rect response ad is working, *keep doing it for Pete's sake!*

I once had a client who was disappointed with a 10 percent rate of re-sponse to his letter. He was expecting an 80 percent or 100 percent re-sponse rate. He could not believe 90 percent did not answer his letter.

I asked him, "How much did the mailing cost?"

Answer: "About $1,200."

I asked: "How much business did the mailing bring in?"

Answer: "Let me think. Hmmmm. About $15,000."

My response to him: "Good Heavens! This is a staggering success. Send the same mailing again to those who did not answer and simply stamp 'SECOND NOTICE' in red on the carrier."

He did as I instructed, and $10,000 in new business came in.

I told him, mail it a third and fourth time and see what happens.

I then suggested he change the look and feel of the package, craft new headlines to make the mailing look different, and make a few changes in the copy; then mail it again. Another $15,000 in new business came in.

If you find something that works, keep doing it until it stops working.

Meanwhile, test other messages and approaches. Soon you'll have an entire arsenal of letters you can mail to your customers and prospects.

On the other hand, if your marketing is not working, if it's not bringing in immediate business, stop doing it immediately and try something else. Don't believe those who tell you to run an ad over and over again that gets no response. Don't believe those who tell you it often takes a long time for an ad to work. That's the Madison Avenue approach. But you and I don't have enough money to conduct saturation advertising and hope that your ads work someday. Your ads must work now.

If your ads, your direct mail, or your Internet marketing campaigns aren't bringing in instant business, stop doing what you are doing immediately; and find a message, a product, an offer and an advertising tool that does bring in instant leads and customers.

If you can't hit a nail without hitting your thumb, don't keep doing what you are doing. Stop. Change your technique. Change your approach. Try something else. Find a direct marking expert to help you analyze what you are doing wrong.

Rule #3
If you try it and it doesn't work, you're doing it wrong.

So often I hear people say "direct mail does not work," or "Internet marketing does not work for me," or "Advertising in the Yellow Pages does not work."

To say these methods don't work just means you're doing something wrong.

Don't tell me direct mail doesn't work. It clearly works, or I would not see so much of it in my mailbox. If Internet marketing did not work, if TV ads did not work, if radio ads did not work, if postcards and newsletters did not work, if the Yellow Pages did not work, people would stop using these media. All these media and methods work. To say they don't work is like saying planes don't work because some crash. That's like saying golf clubs don't work because I can't get the ball to go where I want it to go.

All these marketing media and methods are powerful tools. But you must use the tools correctly. You must learn how to use the tools. You must learn what the tools are supposed to do and what situations and circumstances fit the tools you select.

Please never tell me these tools don't work. They clearly do work. Make it your mission to learn how to use them correctly.

Chapter Seventeen

The nine-step formula for writing successful sales letters

1. **Craft a great first sentence that creates intrigue.**

Leading off your letter with a question is often a good device to engage the reader. Here's a pretty good one:

> "If I can show you how you can double your income in 90 days by giving me just 30 minutes of your time, would you like to learn more?"

Questions can be effective lead sentences because you are immediately engaging your reader in a conversation. You are not preaching at your reader. You are not screaming at your reader. You are not lecturing your reader. You are asking your reader to give her opinion. You are, in effect, putting your reader in charge of the conversation. And you are doing so in a way that gets your reader thinking and imagining.

Another effective attention-getter is to start with a damaging admission. Here's an example:

> If you're looking for a big, prestigious Madison Avenue ad agency to create and conduct your ad campaign, we're not for you.
>
> But if you're looking for an affordable ad agency that knows the local market right here in Palooka, I encourage you to check out our Web site at **AffordableAdAgency.com** to pick up your free report that will give you 10 rules for creating great ads.
>
> Our offices are modest because we don't spend your hard-earned money on mahogany wood

```
paneling, marble floors, fat salaries, and a
fancy address. We use your money to create
affordable and effective ads and marketing
campaigns for you and your business.
```

The damaging admission is a great way to start, because your honesty is disarming. By immediately revealing your weakness, your reader is far more likely to believe your claims. A damaging admission is attention-getting in itself.

Human nature is such that we all start listening intently when someone starts admitting his weaknesses, mistakes, blunders, and disasters. That's a whole lot more interesting than listening to someone prattle on about how great he is.

Or here's another way to start:

```
"I am writing you because it's a matter
of public record that you are having finan-
cial problems, and I think I have a way to
help you."
```

This is attention-getting because you have just told your reader that you know something damaging about him.. You have inside information about your reader. It's a bit of a shocker. Who would not keep reading after being hit on the head with such an opening line? Yikes!

Later, I'll get more deeply into the science of crafting the opening line.

2. Figure out all the benefits of what you are selling and promise your most important benefit first.

Notice that I use the word "benefits," not "features."

People don't buy things or products, people buy great results. People don't buy drills, they buy the holes that drills make. You're not buying leather seats for your car, you're buying comfort, beauty, prestige. Am I selling drivers to golfers, or am I selling long straight shots guaranteed to take your ball an extra 20 yards down the fairway and improve your score?

Before I start writing, I list on index cards all benefits (results) I can identify the product achieving for the prospect. I then organize them in order of priority. I ask others to organize the cards in the priority they think is right. I take a kind of mini-poll—because what I think is important might very well be wrong. The larger your poll sample, the better your data will be. Ask as many people as you can to help you prioritize your benefits index cards.

If you can find a "hidden benefit," that can further strengthen your appeal. Anytime you can share a secret, show people something "hidden," ears will perk up.

A hidden benefit of aspirin is that it helps diminish the likelihood of heart attacks and strokes by thinning the blood and thereby unclogging arteries. Wow, that's a pretty good benefit. We're now supposed to take an aspirin-a-day, whether or not we have a headache. And that's great news for aspirin makers, who were on the ropes because of Tylenol.

A hidden benefit of the time-management program you are selling is that not only will it make you more productive and your business more profitable, but you'll have a lot more time for your family, for golf, and for doing the things you love doing.

In almost every product you sell you can find "hidden benefits" that might be even more attractive than the obvious benefit. "Hidden benefits" are like "hidden treasures." They are so much more exciting to read about.

3. Describe your most important benefit in detail.

Your readers must be persuaded that your claims are true. You must prove your claims.

You do this by going into a fair amount of detail about how and why your product will achieve the wonderful benefit you are describing. You don't do this with a lot of hype. You don't do this by using empty words like "amazing" and "incredible." You do this with facts, reasons, and interesting, little-known details.

The great advertising writer Claude Hopkins, nearly a century ago, was hired by Schlitz beer to craft an ad campaign that would rescue the company. Schlitz at the time was running about fifteenth in beer sales and was in deep trouble.

Hopkins made a trip to Wisconsin to visit the brewery. He needed to learn more about how beer was made. Hopkins knew that it was impossible to sell without a thorough knowledge of the product being sold.

The folks at Schlitz showed Hopkins the entire brewing process, step by step. They showed him how deep they had drilled their wells to find the purest water. They showed him the glass-enclosed rooms that kept the water pure, the kind of yeast they used and where they got it. They showed Hopkins the place where the bottles were cleaned, re-cleaned, and sanitized a dozen times.

"My God," Hopkins said, "Why don't you tell people in your advertising about all these steps you are taking to brew your beer?"

But, answered the Schlitz people, "All companies brew their beer about the same way."

"Yes," Hopkins countered, "but the first one to tell the public about this process will gain a big advantage."

Hopkins then launched an ad campaign for Schlitz that described in detail the company's step-by-step brewing process for making the beer. Within six months, Schlitz jumped to the #1 selling beer.

Here's the text of the legendary Hopkins print ad:

Perfection of 50 Years

Back of each glass of Schlitz beer there is an experience of 50 years. In 1848, in a hut, Joseph Schlitz began brewing. Not like Schlitz beer of today; but it was honest. It was the best beer America had ever brewed.

This great brewer today has new methods. A half-century has taught us perfection. But our principles are 50 years old, our aims are unaltered.

Schlitz beer is still brewed without regard to expense, according to the best that we know.

We send experts to Bohemia to select the best hops in the world.

An owner of the business selects the barley, and buys only the best that grows.

A partner in our concern supervises every stage of the brewing.

> Cleanliness is not carried to greater extremes in any kitchen than here. Purity is made imperative. All beer is cooled in plate glass rooms, in filtered air. The beer is filtered. Then it is sterilized, after being bottled and sealed.
>
> We age our beer for months in refrigerating rooms before it goes out. Otherwise Schlitz beer would cause biliousness, as common beer does.
>
> Ask for beer, and you get the beer that best suits your dealer.
>
> He may care more for his profit than your health. Ask for Schlitz, and you get the best beer the world ever knew.

Notice that Hopkins used no empty "hype" words. His claims are backed up by facts, details, and narrative. If anything, Hopkins' tone is understated, and this contributes to the ad's believability. Hopkins proved with this legendary ad that there are no boring subjects, just boring writers.

"Who wants to hear a story about the step-by-step brewing process of making beer?" one might wonder. Turns out, those who love beer are fascinated by the subject.

They want to know exactly and precisely why they should pick this beer above all others. This great copywriter Claude Hopkins, the father of modern advertising, understood this law of marketing and went on to turn the brewing process into an exciting story, full of detail—and of riveting interest to beer lovers.

Follow the Hopkins formula in all your letter and ad writing. You will do very well.

4. Tell readers specifically what they are going to get.

Your customers want to know exactly what they will be getting for their money.

Again, this is just more of the Claude Hopkins formula.

When you buy a car, you want the exact specifications, so that when you compare prices with other dealers you know you are comparing apples to apples. When you buy a computer, you need to know the specifications: How fast is it? How much memory does it have? How big is the screen? How clear is the resolution?

Include all the information. If the information is highly technical, such as with computers, you should include this on a separate insert, perhaps along with a beautiful and impressive photo of the computer you are selling. Technical specifications make for boring copy, so the complete list should not be included in the letter, just the highlights. But a complete list should be included somewhere.

If you are selling a seminar on tape, or a study-at-home course, you should include an impressive photo of all the materials that will be arriving in a box. Your letter, your sales package, is like a show-and-tell presentation. Provide all the information—if not all in the letter, on separate inserts and enclosures. Give your reader a lot of great material to study.

5. Provide third-party testimony to the truth of your claims.

Anything the salesman has to say is going to be met with skepticism, no matter how compelling your story and your claims, no matter how exact the details you describe.

You need others—preferably famous and respected people—to confirm that what you are saying is true.

If you are selling a fix for muscle pain, you should have endorsements by top doctors—perhaps doctors who work for professional sports teams. An endorsement of your muscle pain cure from the official team doctor of the New York Giants would be impressive.

But it's also important for endorsements not to be just hype.

Endorsements are best if they are mini-stories—a mini-story on how the recognized expert discovered your product and then a fairly detailed description of exactly what your product achieved for him is an effective, believable testimonial.

The more testimonials you have the better. I sometimes include an entire booklet of testimonials with my mailings. I feel I can never have enough testimonials. I also try to secure testimonials on audio and video and put them on my Web site. Sometimes I'll include a CD, DVD, or VHS videotape with my mailing that includes all my testimonials, accompanied by the printed version (because I know many people will not take the time to view the DVD).

6. Tell readers what bad things will happen if they fail to act now.

Your readers must be given good reasons to act now, not tomorrow. People buy more out of impulse. If your prospect puts your letter aside, thinking she will get to it later, your appeal is probably doomed. Your reasons to act now, not tomorrow, must also be credible, not hype. For example:

> The registration deadline for my Direct Marketer's Boot Camp is September 23. I'm limiting enrollment to just 24 people to ensure that each participant receives personal one-on-one coaching, which includes an analysis of your current direct marketing offers.
>
> I am accepting enrollment applications in the order of their arrival. The Boot Camps always fill up long before the deadline date. So I encourage you to send me your application as soon as you possibly can. To enroll immediately, you can also call me at 1.800_____, or enroll online at: **www.website.com.**

Can you see how the reason I give for my reader to answer my letter immediately also restates some of the key benefits of the seminar?

In this case, it is the personal one-on-one coaching and analysis of the customer's current direct marketing offers. I might also mention that "This is the last time I've scheduled a Boot Camp in the Cleveland area. I'm sure I'll be back again, but maybe not for another couple of years."

Suggesting to your reader that this is a "last chance" opportunity to do something or buy something is always strong.

When *Seinfeld*, or *M*A*S*H*, or *Dallas* announced their last and final shows, when we were told there would never be another show made, these last and final programs were some of the most widely watched TV shows in history.

You might not be looking to buy a gun. You might never have thought of buying a gun before. But what if you knew that all gun purchases would be banned after tomorrow? And that after tomorrow, you would never be allowed to buy another gun? You would see a stampede into the gun stores.

"Last chance" arguments for acting now is a proven formula for success. But, as with all your sales letters and presentations, the claim must be believable.

Avoid using shopworn phrases used by amateur writers like "Supplies are limited, so act now." Everyone knows you probably have a warehouse full of the junk. Stronger would be a more credible "We're down to the last few books, and it could be many months before we go back up on press with another printing. So I encourage you to get your order in today. Calling our 1.800 _____. Or ordering online at **www.website.com** is the surest and fastest way to secure your book."

This says almost same thing, but it's far more precise. The reasons are solid. And there's no hype—just good solid facts and reasons for acting now and not waiting until tomorrow.

7. Rephrase the most prominent benefits in the closing and in other parts of the package

Repeating your message is crucial in all successful marketing. But don't repeat the same words all the time or you will bore your reader. Look for new, fresh ways to underscore what your offer is and what the benefits are. This is where thought and creativity come in.

You do this in your lead. You back up your claims in the body of your letter, in the enclosures and testimonials. And you summarize your offer, restating the principal benefit in the P.S. and on the order form.

What you are offering, what you are selling, must be crystal clear in about three seconds. Your reader must never need to search for what you are selling.

8. Include a money-back guarantee

This is absolutely essential, because you are asking your reader, who may never have met you, to trust your claims and send you money. And, as with everything else in your letter, you must make your guarantee believable.

Your reader must feel absolutely certain that this guarantee you are describing is real. It must be unconditional, no questions asked.

The guarantee should be a stand-alone certificate, signed by the letter signer. It should be on nice paper and look something like a stock certificate or a U.S. savings bond. It should look like an official document from the U.S. Treasury. It should look like it has real monetary value just by itself. It should look something like money.

This will grab the attention of your reader and reassure your reader.

You might take your guarantee and assurance of satisfaction one step further. "If you are ever having any problems with this product, please call me directly. The direct line to my desk is _____. If you don't reach me there, my cell phone number is _____."

And you might make this promise: "If you are unhappy in anyway with my service, just write cancel on my invoice and mail it back to me. You'll owe nothing for the month."

Or, "If you ever have a problem that we cannot fix within 24 hours, I'll give you this month's service for free. And you will continue to receive service free until we fix the problem to your satisfaction."

Always put the buyer in charge of the guarantee and the decision as to whether a refund is called for.

9. Offer instant gratification.

In the 21st century, the age of high-speed Internet and overnight delivery, you must offer instant gratification.

People today are not patient. They are not willing to "allow four-to-six weeks for delivery." That's like waiting until the next life.

Be sure always to include a toll-free phone number and Web site order form so they can order immediately. And offer an overnight delivery option. People want their TV programs now, today, not several days from now when the cable hook-up guy can get to it. So when your sales letter is mailed, be sure you are ready to fulfill orders instantly.

Chapter Eighteen
Seventeen reasons people buy . . . plus the #1 reason people buy

1. Fear

People buy because they fear getting old, fear going broke, fear being left behind. They fear being left out. They fear death. They fear getting sick, fear going to Hell, fear being alone. They fear Republicans gaining power, or they fear Democrats gaining power. They fear the Nazis or Communists gaining power. They fear life is meaningless. They fear failure. They fear their kids won't amount to anything. They fear being insignificant, not leaving a mark. Fear comes in all shapes, sizes, and forms. Fear is a powerful motivator causing people to buy.

2. Desire to be recognized

People buy because they want honor and prestige. They want recognition. They want to be set apart from the crowd. They want to be part of an exclusive, prestigious club. They want fame.

3. Greed

Just about everyone wants more money. No matter how rich someone is, they always want more. Even billionaires want more, not because they need it, just because they want it.

They want more than the other billionaire has. Warren Buffet has not stopped trying to make more money even though he's the second richest man in the world. Bill Gates still wants more because he wants to stay the richest.

Ten thousand pairs of shoes were not enough for Imelda Marcos. She always wanted more shoes.

4. Love

Love is a powerful motivator to buy. What other motive can there be for buying life insurance? People want to make sure their children have the best and that their loved ones are taken care of.

5. Self-improvement

People always want to improve themselves. They join a gym to get in shape. They sign up for a seminar to learn something that will help them get ahead. "How To" manuals are some of the best selling books on Amazon.

6. Desire to win

There's a strong competitive instinct in most people. People just flat out want to win at games, at sports, at business, at love, and in life. No one wants to be called a "Loser."

People want to be the best. They want the recognition that goes with winning, or they just want the satisfaction of knowing they are the best at something. It's not enough for Tiger Woods to be the best golfer in the world. He now wants to be the best golfer of all time. Does he want to win because he wants more fame or more money? Does winning make him feel superior to other people? I don't think so. I think he is someone who sets a goal and then just wants to achieve it. He's a perfectionist. He feels he can always do better.

The desire to win will cause people to buy the best equipment, get the best teacher, buy the best books and videos on the subject. We want our kids to win. We want our teams to win. The innate desire most of us have to win fuels the sports industry and much of our economy.

7. Comfort

People want comfort. They want a comfortable bed, a comfortable chair, a comfortable car, comfortable shoes, comfortable clothes. People want a Jacuzzi. We want pain relievers even for the most minor pains, just to make ourselves more comfortable. We want larger and more comfortable rooms. Americans, especially, seem to be on a never-ending quest for more and more comfort.

8. Laziness

Sure, people want to improve themselves, and they want to win, and they want to make more money . . . but only if it's easy.

People are lazy. That's why you don't see many sales pitches that highlight how hard you must work to achieve the results being advertised. You will see beautiful people sitting on the exercise equipment and talking more often than we see them actually use it. People want the results without the work. "Lose 10 pounds in 30 days with no dieting or exercise. Just take this pill." That's the basic pitch.

9. Quest for a great experience

People want great experiences they will remember for the rest of their lives. They want travel experiences, educational experiences, family outings, parties, vacations, barbecues, great food at great restaurants, and good movies to watch. They want exciting experiences, relaxing experiences, social experiences, and entertainment experiences. People want shared experiences with loved ones. The travel and entertainment industry is all about creating and selling memorable experiences.

10. Sex

People want more sex and better sex. People want sex, period. People want to be more attractive and sexier. Sex is everywhere in advertising, movies, and entertainment. Sometimes it's in the open, sometimes implied. The mere mention of the word "sex" draws immediate and riveted attention.

11. The desire for relationships

People want friends. People want dates. People want romance. People want to get married. People want to be connected to other people.

People want to be part of a community. Dating sites are among the most popular on the Internet. People want to improve their relationships with their children and with their spouse. When a relationship breaks up, it's painful. When a relationship starts, it's exciting. Most people do not want to be alone in the world.

12. Anger

Anger can be a very strong motivator. People send money to the Republican Party because they are angry at the Democrats. People send money to the Democratic Party because they are angry at the Republicans. People hire a lawyer to sue someone because they are angry. Following the 9/11 terrorist attack on America, people bought flags and decals not just out of patriotism, but also to show their anger at the terrorists. That was certainly justified anger. Anger makes people want to strike back and fight, even go to war.

13. Desire to make a difference

People want their lives to count for something, to make a difference.

People run for President and public office to make a difference—hopefully not just for recognition. People contribute to charities, political causes, and religious organizations to make a difference. People become teachers and religious leaders to make a difference. People write books and articles to make a difference. People volunteer to make a difference.

Very few people want their life to count for absolutely nothing, to have made no positive impact in the world. Most people want to leave a legacy of some kind.

The desire to have an impact, to leave a mark, to make the world a better place, can be a powerful motivator to buy or contribute.

14. Desire for meaning in life

People want life to mean something. Religious organizations rely on this motive to prosper. Most people believe in God. Most people do not want to believe their life is an accident. People buy Bibles, religious tracts, and philosophical discourses to find meaning in life. They join a church and attend seminars for the same reason.

Billions of dollars are spent every year by people wanting to find meaning in life.

15. Desire for power

People want to tell others what to do. They want to be in charge. They want power. They want to be like God. Sometimes they want power to do good things, sometimes evil things.

Elections are about deciding who will be in charge. Billions of dollars are spent to win elections, win power. People start their own businesses and organizations in part because they want to be the boss. People want to be in charge of their own lives and in charge of other people's lives as well.

Serial killers are the way they are because they want power over others—their victims. The desire for power over others is at the root of every war. The obsession for power has caused enormous human misery: Hitler, Stalin, Mao Tse Tung, Pol Pot, and countless dictators throughout history. Thank heavens in America we have found a way to prevent anyone from getting too much power.

The desire for power is one of the most powerful human motives.

16. Necessity of life

People need food, water, soap, clothes, electricity, gas, transportation, haircuts, phones. Maybe computers and Internet connections now fall under the category of a necessity of modern life. Businesses need paper, copiers, desks, chairs, fax machines, phones, and computers.

"Can't do without it" is certainly a powerful reason to buy.

17. Addiction

People become addicted to drugs, alcohol, tobacco, caffeine, gambling, pornography, sex, and fast food. Some addictions are physical, other psychological. But the effect is the same, an ever-present compulsion to get more. Marketers of these products see their jobs as feeding the addiction and creating more addicts to the substance, product, or activity. This is how the drug dealers, the tobacco and alcohol companies, the porn industry, sex traffickers, the casinos, and the fast food and junk food companies are making billions.

The #1 reason people buy

In the previous section I listed seventeen motives fueling the desire of people to buy something. But almost all of these can be recast and placed under one motive.

The most powerful motive of all is **fear.**

People are very insecure about their place in life.

Are people searching for love, or are they more afraid of ending up alone?

Stopping something bad from happening is always a more powerful motivator than causing something good to happen. I exercise not so I can look like Mr. Universe, but because I fear looking like Jabba the Hut. I want to make more money not so I can buy more things, but mostly to guard against going broke.

Desire for power is a subset of fear. So is anger. People are angry because they are not in control. Short people (i.e., Hitler, Stalin, Napoleon, Mao Tse Tung, Pol Pot) seem more interested in power than tall people (Thomas Jefferson, George Washington).

People want power and get angry mostly because they are insecure—which is a variation of the fear motive.

Your sales letters will perform far better if you talk about, or imply, all the bad things that will happen to your reader if he fails to answer your letter. If you receive a letter from the IRS or an attorney, you are very likely to open it—far more likely than a letter from Bloomingdales.

People fear the IRS, fear lawsuits, fear getting older, fear dying, fear failing, fear loneliness, fear nature, fear getting sick, fear God, fear going to Hell, fear being left behind or left out, fear being fired, fear not keeping up with the Joneses, fear not amounting to anything in life, fear for their kids, fear not being understood, fear other people, fear walking down the street, and just generally fear life. Woody Allen built a career of making movies about people's fears, insecurities, and neuroses.

The news media sells almost nothing but fear, because news organizations know that fear sells.

Rarely do we hear a positive news story. Mostly we hear stories about disasters, crimes, wars, typhoons, and disease. People contribute to causes mostly because they want to stop something bad from happening.

How does the car salesman stop you from walking out of the showroom?

> "Another guy also loved this car and says he'll be back later today with his down payment. If you don't buy it now, this car will be gone this evening."

Or . . .

> "This deal I'm offering you expires at the end of the month, which is today. We're actually losing money on this price. We're only offering this price today so we can meet our sales quota for the month because if we meet our quota, we get a bonus from GM."

I'm sure you've heard these or similar pitches before.

The salesman is using fear (your fear of losing out) as a way to persuade you to make an immediate decision. People buy not so much to gain something, but because they fear losing something important if they don't buy now.

Chapter Nineteen
The Offer

A **great offer can** succeed with very poor copy.

But the best copy in the world cannot sell a poor offer.

This is another way of saying, "People are not idiots." They count their pennies. They make mathematical calculations before parting with their hard-earned money. They want the best deal. If they find a better deal somewhere else, they'll take it.

The challenge is constructing an irresistible offer that won't bankrupt you. If I said, "Here, have a free Ferrari," you would certainly take it and not believe your good fortune. But that would not make much business sense for me.

Price

Price is a critical consideration in constructing your offer. Your price must be high enough so as to allow sufficient mark-up, while not so high as to discourage buyers. What is your ideal price to charge? Industry standard is one way to measure. I always prefer testing—trial and error.

Shipping and handling

Do you include it in the price of your product? Or do you pad some profit in your shipping and handling charge? Shipping and handling is a significant cost.

Unit of sale

Are you selling one at a time? A "two for the price of one" deal? Do you offer a bulk rate discount? This will depend on the product you are selling and test results.

You might want to keep your offer simple and just offer one unit. You risk confusing your reader by offering too many options.

Offering choices often depresses sales. Plus, selling one unit at a time might allow you to capture more customers, which might be more important than moving a lot of this particular product. So decide what your primary goal is and drive toward that target. Don't try to achieve more than one objective with your sales piece.

Options and extras

It's usually best to highlight only the basic price of the product in your advertising, and then sell additional options and extras after the customer has made a decision to buy the basic product. You'll never see an ad for a car with the price of the car as it would be fully loaded. The price advertised is usually the lowest it can possibly be without any "extras." The extras are sold at the point of sale. "Would you like leather seats? How about cruise control and electric windows?" All this is extra and adds to the basic price.

The up-sell

This is a little different from the options and extras listed above. With this approach you reel in your customer with your lower-priced product and, on the phone or in person, attempt to sell him a more expensive product or an additional related product. You're in the golf store buying a sand wedge. The salesman says, "Would you like to try this incredible driver?" You're at McDonald's buying a quarter-pounder, "Would you also like some fries? How about a drink? Have you tried our new Oreo cookie shake?"

Over time, you will learn what percentage of customers you can up-sell. This will increase the value of your average customer.

And this will change your calculations as to how much you can spend to acquire a customer. The up-sell potential can affect how you calculate your initial offer.

Future obligation

"Choose any of these four best-selling books and pay just 10 cents, and agree to buy four more over the next 12 months."

This offer is common for book clubs and tape/CD/DVD clubs. These offers require the seller to take a short-term loss in exchange for a long-term payoff.

Pay over time

If you are selling an expensive item, offering the option of paying in monthly installments is often a good idea. Consumers have become used to automatic monthly charges being billed to their credit card. $395 for an item is a hefty check for a consumer to write all at once. But $32.91 charged each month for 12 months to a credit card or debit card sounds like about what I might be paying for my gym membership or cable TV bill. It's a lot more palatable and won't stand out on my monthly credit card billing statement.

The "Bill Me Later" option is often used for subscription offers. Sellers of big-ticket durable items, such as furniture and washing machines, will sometimes hype "No payments for a year."

Most of us would much rather pay later than pay now and pay monthly rather than pay all at once.

Free trial

Here's an approach you might try with the right product:

> "Your three-month trial subscription is free. If you decide *National Review* magazine is not for you, just write "Cancel" on the 12-month subscription invoice we'll be sending you in 90 days after your three-month trial subscription has run out."

No fee, 0% interest rate

No annual fee is typical of credit card offers. If you read the fine print, what you will find is the "no annual fee" offer is usually replaced by a higher interest rate. Or if there's a 0% interest rate offered, it's an introductory interest rate and will soon go up to ordinary levels, or possibly extraordinary levels.

You'll sometimes see 0% financing for offers by auto dealers. This is an eye-catcher, but just understand that the cost of offering a 0% interest rate must be captured somewhere else: higher price for the car, bigger down payment requirement. But these can be effective offers, mostly because they are eye-catching.

Pre-approved

This is another staple of credit card marketing. What the marketer is telling us is that there will be no hard work involved getting this card — no pain-in-the neck application to fill out. Just tell us you want the card and we'll send it to you.

This approach is also taken by retailers who offer special store credit cards that are good only in that store.

Mail-in rebate

The mail-in cash rebate offer allows the marketer to hype a lower price, a tactic that is often used by sellers of computers, software, televisions, and electronics equipment. The ad will hype the price of the computer as **"$850** after your $100 cash rebate."

So you still have to pay $950 for the computer, and then jump over all kinds of hurdles and wait for weeks, even months for your $100 to be refunded. Many of these companies make it so difficult to get the cash rebate that buyers just give up. You have to mail in your receipt (the original, not a copy), cut the bar code off the carton, find the serial number of the product, write the name and address of the store where you bought the product, list the name of the salesman, and then wait eight weeks. You will then likely get a notice telling you no rebate is coming because you missed some step. You then have no chance of fixing the problem because you've already sent them your original receipt and bar code from the carton.

I'm not a fan of the rebate tactic because most often it's a lie. The price hyped in the ad is really not the price.

Free gift

Enclosing a free gift with your sales letter is a good way to draw attention to your letter and to illustrate what you are selling.

If you're in the office product supply business, sending your customers and prospects a pocket calendar or a pen with the name, address, and phone number of the store printed on it can work well. Giving away coffee mugs that advertise your business can also be a nice touch. And there's a chance your coffee mug, with your business's name prominently displayed, will stay on your prospect's desk all year, or at least be stored with all his other coffee mugs and seen on occasion.

I have enclosed nice coffee mugs and cups with my sales appeals to great effect. The free gift gets attention for my letter, and the coffee cup, especially if it's one of those nice thermal ones that keeps your coffee warm and fits well into a coffee cup holder in a car, is appreciated.

If you develop an especially nice and useful free gift, this can actually become part of your brand. One fellow I know who runs a non-profit organization is a beekeeper as a hobby. He sends a jar of honey from his beehives every year to his best donors. This is the kind of thoughtful free gift everyone who receives it remembers and appreciates. It sure works well for him.

Perhaps the best use of the free gift is the free toy McDonald's gives away with its Happy Meals. The little kids are more interested in the toy than the meal. What McDonald's is doing is hooking kids on fast food at an early age with the toy. The kids then drag their parents to McDonald's so the kids can get the toy. It's a brilliant marketing strategy, using the kids to get parents to bring the entire family to McDonald's, trips that then become lifelong memories—family traditions. It's also why Americans are getting so fat, but that's a topic outside the scope of this book.

The free prize in Cracker Jack is another example, as is the comic in Bazooka Joe bubble gum and the secret decoder ring hidden in the kids' cereal box. The point is: skillful use of the free gift for the right products can significantly boost your response. People just love gifts and prizes.

Free extras

If you are selling a subscription to a newsletter or magazine, your offer will almost always do better if you add several free extras, such as a free special report and free book.

These free extras should be precisely on point with the main product you are selling. Don't throw in a free toaster with your newsletter subscription offer.

Infomercials will always toss in plenty of free extras, often as incentives for responding immediately. Sometimes the free extras sound more appealing than the main product. In addition to this miracle knife, "you will get this set of six beautiful steak knives absolutely free if you call this number today, plus you will receive . . . You will also receive . . . And here's another thing you will get . . ."

The impression the offer leaves is that you will be showered with a lot of valuable free stuff if you call right now.

Incentives

Banks and credit card companies want you to use their credit card and not someone else's. So they offer incentives. You might get frequent flier miles—attractive if you fly a lot.

So this is an offer made most to affluent people who travel often, either on business or for vacation. Discover offers "cash back" for using its card. This probably appeals more to lower income folks who place greater value on having a few extra bucks in their pocket.

American Express lets you select items from a product catalogue if you rack up enough "rewards points."

I don't like this offer much. I never have time to go through the catalogue and it seems you have to rack up an awful lot of points to qualify for anything worthwhile.

I like frequent flier miles. This offer is putting the beleaguered airline industry under financial pressure, so they keep putting more and more restrictions on how frequent flier miles can be used.

Sweepstakes

Reader's Digest **builds** its subscription list almost entirely with a sweepstakes offer. Publisher's Clearing House offers subscriptions to many different magazines with its sweepstakes contest. With the sweepstakes offer, the main event is the sweepstakes contest, while the subscription offer is the sideshow.

Sweepstakes contests work best for low-priced items. And the items must be useful to everyone. *Reader's Digest* is the kind of magazine that anyone would enjoy. A sweepstakes offer would not work as well for selling a specialty publication.

Sweepstakes offers only work well when mailed to lists built by other sweepstakes offers. There is a segment of the population that is fanatical about playing sweepstakes contests. They will play just about every sweepstakes contest they can get their hands on.

And if the product seems worthwhile, they will throw a few bucks into the reply envelope to buy it. It's an impulse purchase, like picking up a packet of Gummy Bears while going through the checkout line at the supermarket. You don't go into the store expecting to buy Gummy Bears, but you saw them sitting there, so grabbed a packet. That's basically how the sweepstakes contest works.

There is also a nagging suspicion in the back of the mind of the sweepstakes player that buying the product, whatever it is, might improve the odds of winning. Even though the letter and the copy throughout the sweepstakes package is very clear that buying will not improve the odds of winning, that all responders have an equal chance of winning whether they buy or not, some sweeps players still believe buying the product will improve their chance of winning. And if the product looks useful anyway, there's no harm in buying it if it only costs a few bucks.

Sweepstakes offers have become increasingly popular on the Internet as an incentive for people to supply their email address, and perhaps also to fill out a survey. What the sweepstakes sponsor is doing is collecting valuable marketing information on the sweeps players so they can come back at them later with more precisely-targeted sales pitches.

* * *

The writing and creative work cannot begin until you have decided the offer. How much can you spend to acquire a customer? How good a deal can you really afford to offer? What is the likely long-term value of the average new customer to you?

These are critical questions you must answer when constructing your offer. And you must constantly test offers and combinations of offers.

Chapter Twenty
The critical importance of "positioning"

"Positioning" is the most critical issue to settle before you begin your marketing and before you construct offers to test.

And the reason is this:

An offer is not just about price and terms.

Sometimes if you charge too little, people value your service less. If your surgeon was only charging you $25 per hour for his work, you might appreciate his low price, but you would certainly decline his service. "How can he charge so little if he's any good?" you would think.

On the other hand, if he's charging you $500 per hour, you might stagger at the price, but accept it, knowing his price is high because he's the very best at what he does, and you certainly want the very best surgeon operating on you.

Are Gucci's shoes and handbags really worth the staggering price? Are Gucci's products really that much better than other brands that are one-third the price? Gucci's products look pretty flimsy to me. Gucci's entire marketing appeal is that its products are ridiculously over-priced. Apparently, that's part of what people want when they buy Gucci. The Gucci label shouts to their friends: "Look at me! See how much I paid for this. I must have so much money I don't know what to do with it all."

I don't understand this desire people have to advertise to everyone that they've spent too much on a handbag. "I've just been ripped off" is what these people are telling me. But there it is—Gucci's entire marketing pitch in a nutshell.

Diamonds are not really rare stones at all. But DeBeers has figured out how to create a near monopoly on the production and supply of diamonds. Then DeBeers figured out how to market diamonds not just as rare, but as a way for men to show their love for a woman. "A diamond is forever." Actually, diamonds are common.

So the question of price is not necessarily always about how low the price is compared to your competitors, but about the "positioning" of your product in people's minds. The question of how you "position" your product or service is the most important issue you must settle before you begin your marketing efforts.

Gucci is not really selling shoes and handbags. Gucci is selling image and status. DeBeers is not really selling clear, sparkling stones. DeBeers is selling "proof that he loves me."

Figure out your Unique Selling Proposition—U.S.P.

What is it that's different about your business, your product, your service? What is it that your product does that no other product does?

What makes you different from your competitors?

We marketers toss around the term "unique selling proposition" all the time. But I've found very few small businesses that can tell me in 50 words or less why I or any other consumer should buy from them as opposed to all the other choices I have.

All this takes is a little thought and creativity.

Maybe what makes you different is that you are local. Or maybe you're different because you're national. Maybe your advantage is that you're small, or that you're big. Maybe your advantage is that your staff is old and "experienced" or that your staff is young and "energetic."

If I were to start a competitor to the National Rifle Association, I would not start an organization that does exactly what the NRA does. I would try to figure out what needs to be done in the Second Amendment arena that the NRA isn't doing. I would try to find a task that needs doing that no one else is working on.

Perhaps I would try to be even more hardcore and purest on the Second Amendment issue than the NRA. By taking this approach, I would never become as big as the NRA, but I might become 20 percent or 10 percent the size of the NRA.

I would try to find some niche to dominate and become known for, some niche not occupied by the NRA. It would be hopeless to try to compete directly with the NRA, as hopeless as it would be to try to compete with Coca-Cola by launching an imitation cola.

Yes, other companies have done it. Pepsi did it successfully with many billions of dollars in advertising. Of course, Pepsi is unlikely ever to surpass Coke. Pepsi will always be the #2 cola drink, at least in our lifetimes, and that's not bad. But even Pepsi emphasizes its differences with Coke. Pepsi is "less syrupy," has a "cleaner, more refreshing taste," "is chosen by 70 percent of people in blind taste tests," and is for a "younger generation"—or so the company claims.

Pepsi never says it is the same as Coke, but rather claims to taste better than Coke.

But most of us don't have billions of dollars to compete with the Coca-Colas of the world, so we need to do something different, something that's clearly not being done by some other organization that's a lot bigger and richer than we are.

So figure out, or manufacture, what makes you different from your competition, and hammer your theme into the minds of your customers and potential customers with relentless repetition. Of course, your USP must be a difference that's both needed and sellable. No point in having a USP no one wants, like diet pizza.

Chapter Twenty-One
How to write a great sales letter

Sell just one thing

Never try to sell two things in a direct mail package or sales presentation. The mind can grasp one thing at most. You would never want to say, "From me, you can buy a BMW or toothpaste."

Sell one product, one service. And be as specific as possible. Specialists make more money than generalists. Neurosurgeons make more money than general practitioners. The more narrow your focus, the better defined you will be. People want a plumber to fix their plumbing problem, not a jack-of-all-trades handyman.

Narrow is the gate to paradise. Focus your message like a laser. And keep it simple.

By the way, catalogues are not an exception to this rule.

Catalogues, of course, sell more than one thing. They sell many different items. But successful catalogues are really selling one overarching idea or theme. Successful catalogues sell one image, one theme, one concept. And all the products should fit into that theme, or USP.

So, in the final analysis, even catalogues must sell a single, narrow overarching theme to be successful, and not try to be all things to all people (for example, Sharper Image, LL Bean, Lands' End). The more a catalogue company diverts from its single easy-to-understand theme and tries to become all things to all people, the quicker it will fail—for example, Sears.

Give away your ideas and products

This is a theme I come back to over and over again because I believe it's so important.

Don't be afraid to give away your products and ideas for free.

If what you are selling is good, especially if it's really great, give your ideas and products away. Your customers won't be able to get enough.

How do drug dealers create drug addicts? They give the stuff away—for a while. If a company launches a new brand of coffee, they give it away—for a while. If you were to launch a new sport that no one had heard of, you would let people experience it for free—for a while.

Your sales letters, proposals, and sales materials are show-and-tell presentations. So you will need to give away some valuable information. Sure, some of your prospects will steal your ideas and not pay you for them. That's just the cost of doing business. There are some people out there who want whatever they can get for free—the "something for nothing crowd." But you will also find gold out there, those who will appreciate you for your work and what you can do and who will be more than happy to pay you.

My #1 rule for success in business is to focus not on your own problems and your own needs, but on helping others fix their problems. If you do that well, your problems will be fixed along the way. So don't worry that some of your prospects will just rip-off your ideas and some of your services and not pay you for them.

My response to that is simply to say, "Glad I helped." And isn't it best if you find out early what people are like early, rather than find out later when they might owe you a lot of money?

The importance of headlines

Headlines are absolutely essential for grabbing the attention of the reader. Headlines are what people read to see if they have any interest in what you have to say.

The headline writers at the *New York Post* and *National Inquirer* are masters of the craft. People buy these newspapers entirely because of the headlines. And people read the articles because they want the details that justify such amazing headlines.

Headline writing is critical in all sales and marketing copy. Here are some fill-in-the-blank headline formulas that you might find useful.

"21 Rules for Writing Headlines That Sell"

"Seven Predictions for 2008 that can Change Your Life"

"Eleven secrets of successful investing"

"I lost 10 pounds in 10 days"

"How moving to Nevada saved my company
$1,000,000 the first year"

"How I slashed $50,000 off my income tax bill"

"How I'm able to spend my day at the office in the nude"

"Why I'll never let my kids sit in a classroom"

"The #1 Mistake Made By Parents"

"Why my 10-year old boy would rather read a
book than watch TV"

"How I beat cancer by knowing what questions to
ask my doctor"

"How I solved my sex problems without Viagra
or any other drug"

"How I put excitement back in my marriage"

"How I got my wife to stop nagging me and
start praising me"

"How I motivated myself to get in shape"

"How you can look like this and never lift a weight"

"If you like to write, I can teach you how to make
$30,000 a month from home"

"WARNING: _____"

"WARNING: 138,000 middle managers just like you will lose their jobs in 2008"

"WARNING: The company you work for has already spent your retirement"

"WARNING: You will probably be sued for everything you're worth within the next 36 months"

"WARNING: The Stock Market Will Drop 30%"

"How to Stop Your Divorce"

"How to Double Your Dating"

"35 rules for staying in the lives of your kids when they grow up"

Can you see the pattern?

These headlines are aimed at hooking the reader.

Notice that nearly every one of these headlines taps into a fear or an anxiety people have. The word "secret" is an attention-getter. People want secrets. I would like to know the secret to a consistent golf swing that will produce consistently straight shots.

The word "hidden" is another word that triggers interest. People want to know where the "hidden" treasure is. Hidden implies almost no one knows about it. I just need a map. I just need someone to tell me where this "hidden" treasure is.

"How To . . ." and "How I . . ." are often good ways to start a headline. Also numbering the ways or items in your headline can be effective: "Seven Habits of Successful People." A number suggests that the program is limited, definable, achievable. "If I do these seven things, I will be successful. I just need to complete the program," are the thoughts we try to trigger here.

And notice, too, that the headlines always create mystery and intrigue, telling the casual reader what the big benefit is without giving away any answers. The headline tells the reader, "Here's what this letter is about. But you'll need to read it to find the answer to your problem and to satisfy your desire."

By the way, your letter should include some actual answers. Some professional direct mail sales letter writers make the mistake of having their entire letter be almost nothing but headlines and intriguing statements with no real answers.

Your letter does need to deliver the goods, or your reader will just be frustrated. Your reader will see you as just another skilled huckster, probably with nothing much of real value to offer.

Never be afraid to give away some of your product. Those who like it will want more. In addition, they will trust you.

Write as people actually speak in everyday life

In your marketing letters, use regular conversational language.

Don't write as your high school English teacher or your college English professor would want you to write.

Write as people actually speak when having a conversation on a street corner. I write my letters as I would write to my mom or a close friend. I now write at a sixth grade level, not because people are unintelligent, but because people simply don't have the time or patience to figure out what I am trying to say.

They don't have time to unscramble the King's English.

Your mission is not to impress your reader with your intelligence. Your mission as a sales writer is to communicate your message as simply and directly as possible.

Always maintain the personal tone of your letter. Instead of saying "we" or "us" use the word "I." Letters should be one-on-one communications.

The phrase "you and I" can be found throughout all my letters. It can sound redundant at times, but the "you and I" phrase is essential for making letters sound personal.

I think the best direct marketing copywriters are people with blue-collar backgrounds who are used to talking with longshoremen, construction workers, and people at sports bars (where I like to hang out). The best direct marketing copywriters are not people with Ivy League educations, or even any college education. A salesman who sells vacuum cleaners door to door and is used to talking with housewives everyday about his product would likely make an excellent direct marketing copywriter.

A direct marketing copywriter need not be able to deliver an esoteric lecture to a room full of college professors. In fact, anyone who can do that should probably select a field other than direct mail or direct marketing copywriting. A sales copywriter must know how to have a casual conversation with average, everyday folks who have everyday concerns and problems.

Write a package, not just a letter

The letter is the heart of your direct mail package.

The letter is certainly the most important element of your package. But your package contains other key components, including an order form or reply form and a carrier envelope at a bare minimum.

I almost always include a variety of inserts, perhaps photographs, testimonials, a certificate highlighting the money-back guarantee, perhaps some kind of lift note, a manila folder full of press clippings on the product, a FAQ booklet, maybe even a CD, DVD, or VHS video tape.

Your direct mail marketing piece is a show-and-tell presentation.

These principles apply to your Internet letters as well.

No matter what element of the package the reader picks up, the reader should be hit over the head with the same message. Never have different messages and different themes conveyed with your inserts.

With every direct mail offer, you must market one and only one concept, one Big Idea. Keep your message simple and focused. The purpose of every element of the package is to underscore the one single overarching reason you are writing.

Some inserts can reinforce different aspects of the one Big Idea you are selling. For example, testimonials and track records show the reader that your product has a history of achieving all the great things you are claiming.

But testimonials and track records must be directly on point with the theme of your letter. If the focus of your organization is finding a cure for cancer, don't insert a track record on your success with assisting hospitalized veterans.

Any insert or enclosure that is off point, even slightly, will distract and confuse your readers, can undermine your credibility, and will depress returns.

Generate emotion

People buy more from impulse than from careful analysis of all facts. They buy it because they want it. Sure, you need facts, arguments, reasons, and logic. But these things alone will leave the reader feeling cold.

Most great salesmen not only know their product thoroughly, they are excited about their product; they have stories to tell about folks who have bought the product and the great things the product has done for them. Great salesmen are likeable, believable people who are comfortable talking with longshoremen, housewives, doctors, or college professors. Great salesmen are happy, optimistic people. Their enthusiasm is genuine and contagious. People like to be around them.

Let's say you are selling what we usually think is a drab product, let's say electronic equipment. Now, what most people will tell you they care about most is, "Will it work and is the price good?" Until recently, most computers were packaged in functional, not especially attractive, gray boxes. Most computers looked pretty much the same.

But then Apple Computers did something that helped its computers fly off the shelves. Apple started putting its computers in attractive brightly-colored boxes. Apple changed the packaging of its computers. Apple theorized that people not only want their computers to work, they also want their computers to look good, to look hip. Computers today have become a form of jewelry. When people take their laptops out at Starbucks to start typing away, they want their computers to look cool, snazzy, zippy, high tech. Even the appearance of electronic equipment counts and can dramatically affect sales. Apple tapped into the "feelings" side of the brain.

How do you do this in print?

All kinds of ways.

You can do it with a challenge, perhaps even vaguely insulting your reader:

> "When are you going to finally
> get tired enough of being fat to do
> something about it?"

This will certainly create an emotional response, and might be the right approach for selling gym memberships.

Here's another approach:

> Three years ago I buried my eight-year-old son Jimmy.
>
> He was killed when he got his hands on a neighbor's handgun that was not properly stored and locked. The gun was loaded, went off and killed my son.
>
> I have dedicated the last three years of my life to developing a gun safe that can only be opened with a handprint, the handprint of the owner of the gun.
>
> I am not at all anti-gun.
>
> I believe strongly in the Second Amendment. But I also believe that with rights come responsibilities. We gun owners have a duty to make sure our guns are stored safely.
>
> I am convinced that this safe can make gun-owner homes safe homes for children, and will help prevent more tragedies, such as happened in our family.

Can you see how an approach like this does not rely on hype and screaming at the reader?

Emotion is created by the details, the facts, and the story. Note also that the writer is very clear that he is not anti-gun-owner—essential when selling a product to gun-owners.

Skillful story telling, carefully selected and choreographed details generate emotion and feeling, cause your reader to pay close attention, and set the stage for getting the order.

Seven words or less

Approach all your direct mail letters, ads, and marketing materials with this thought in mind:

If you can't sum up your basic message in one seven-word (or shorter) sentence, your letter, your sales pitch is probably doomed. You should ask yourself: "Can I fit my central message on a bumper sticker?" If not, stop writing. You'll be wasting your time and money.

The people you're writing to are very busy. They receive a lot of mail every day. They're thinking about things other than the product or service you're writing about. You need to get their attention. If you can't convey your message or offer in about three seconds, your letter is headed for the circular file. Don't ask your reader to try to figure out what you're trying to say.

You must be able to convey your main message instantly with headlines, on your reply form, in your P.S., and in the first sentence of your letter. These are the places your readers will glance at first to decide whether they should keep reading or pitch your letter in the trash.

The all-important start of your letter

The first line is the most important line in the letter—in fact, in the entire package. I will sometimes think for hours, even days about the all-important first line.

If I have the right first line, very often the rest of the letter is easy to write. It almost seems to write itself. Every sentence flows so easily if you've started with the right first sentence.

You know you've chosen the wrong first sentence if the rest of the letter is very difficult to write. In fact, if your letter is difficult to write, chances are it will be difficult for your reader to understand. You should probably just stop writing and go back to the drawing board.

The first sentence is like the foundation upon which you build a house. If the foundation is wrong, the entire structure will collapse.

The all-important job of the first sentence is to interest your reader enough that she continues to read your letter. Your first sentence must be so captivating that it's more difficult to stop reading than to keep reading.

That's no easy task. Here are some approaches I use:

1. The damaging admission

I have never been more upset with myself than when I started reading this book.

That's because I now know I have wasted half of my working life pursuing a wrong approach to my business and professional life.

But the good news is it was not too late to change my strategy.

* * *

I have not had much success working with Fortune 500 companies.

That's because I have little patience with meetings, bureaucracy, and the snail-like pace at which decisions are made.

I work best with entrepreneurs and small business people who are as impatient as I am, and who demand immediate results.

* * *

If an idiot like me can write ads that take in more than $50,000, then I'm betting you can too.

* * *

If a person of average intelligence like me can earn $400,000 a year sitting in my boxer shorts on the couch tapping away on my laptop computer keyboard, I'll bet you can too.

2. A startling, frightening statement

If your child is still lagging behind his peers in school by the fourth grade, he will likely lag behind his peers for the rest of his life.

Now is the time to take action if you think your child is falling behind.

* * *

If you are 15 pounds overweight, the odds are your life will be 10 years shorter.

3. The proposition

- "If you will give me just 30 minutes of your time a month, I will show you how to double your income in less than a year."

- "If you are a non-smoker, you can save 50% a year on life insurance."

- "If your firm needs temporaries, we'll give you your first temp for free."

- "If you've written a book, we'll show you how to get it published."

- "If you'll give me a few minutes of your time, I'll show you how to collect from Social Security no matter what your age."

4. A question that engages the reader

- "If I could show you how you can add 20 yards to your drive in just six swings, would you be interested?"

- "Did you know there are still some people who do not know that . . .?"

- "Do you fear public speaking?"

5. A question that puts your reader on the spot

- "How much do you love your family? Enough to make sure they are financially secure in the event something happens to you?"

- "Are you ashamed of the smells in your kitchen?"

- "Are you embarrassed to try for high-paying jobs because of your poor vocabulary?"

- "What step will you take first if your profits drop this year by 15%?"

- "Are you respected by your employees, or do they laugh at you behind your back?"

- "Does your low income embarrass you?"

6. Breaking news

- "I have just finished attending a conference of the world's leading oncologists, and I have some news for you about the latest treatments for cancer."

- "Because of your excellent credit rating, we are raising your credit limit to $25,000."

- "Congratulations. You have been admitted to Harvard."

7. The mysterious preview

"If you will just give me six minutes
of your time and read my entire letter,
I expect it will be the most profitable
six minutes of your life."

8. Reliance on experts

- "What do doctors use when they have
  headaches?"

- "What does Tiger Woods do when his swing
  goes off track?"

- "As the team doctor for the New York
  Yankees, _____is what I give the
  players for their muscle aches."

9. Rooting for the underdog

- "They laughed when they saw me strap
  on a snowboard, but not when they saw
  me come down the mountain like a
  pro."

- "They chuckled when I volunteered to
  test my skills against my judo teacher,
  but their laughs turned to amazement
  when he was lying on the mat."

10. Riveting story that can be told instantly

"Three years ago, my wife died of lung
cancer. Had I known then what I know now,
she would still be alive."

11. Bestow honor

- "Congratulations! Because of your outstanding record as a_____, you have been awarded . . ."

- "Because of your excellent credit rating, you are among a handful of people who are being awarded a Platinum Card."

12. Prestigious invitation

- "Congratulations! Because of your exemplary academic record at Jefferson High School, you have been nominated by your teacher, Mrs. Joan Smith, to be a delegate to the National Young Leaders Conference in Washington, D.C., this fall."

- "Because you are a key leader in law enforcement, you are invited to participate in the White House Conference on Counter-Terrorism."

- "Congressman Jim Smith requests the honor of your presence at _____."

14. Free gift incentive to act now

- "I have two tickets to the Yankees-Red Sox for you, but I'll need to know by Tuesday if you can use them."

- "You've won a free trip for two to Las Vegas. It includes non-stop airfare and two nights at the spectacular Mirage hotel. All you have to do is call by Thursday, May 23, to pick up your e-tickets and hotel reservation confirmation number."

13. Attention-getting enclosure

- "I have enclosed this $1 bill both to get your attention for my letter and to highlight how much it will cost you to become a 21st Century Broadband home for 60 days."

- "I have enclosed this DVD for you because I knew you would not otherwise believe your son can learn the fundamentals of baseball in just seven days at my camp."

- "I am sending you this $10,000 check made payable to RST that will allow you to pay for your first mailing with RST."

- "I am sending you a free signed copy of my new book which I hope you will read before you arrive at my seminar on October 12."

- "I have enclosed a check in the amount of your first month's car payment. Just bring it to me before August 1 for your free test drive of the new _____."

14. Action and involvement

- "If you will complete the enclosed survey and mail it back to me by July 3, I will send you my new book."

- "You have been specially selected to participate in the enclosed survey for Congress on the threat of . . ."

- "I hope you have the courage to Test your I.Q. online by going to IQTest.com to see if you might qualify to . . ."

- "I encourage you to complete the enclosed application to see if you might qualify to enroll in The Screenplay Writers Institute."

Notice that many of these sentences combine techniques and strategies, and they could be put in more than one of these categories. To write powerful leads, first, tap into as many emotions and desires as you possibly can. Then get to, or at least hint at, what you are offering or the opportunity you are presenting, while at the same time creating enough intrigue and mystery so that your reader has little choice but to keep reading.

Can you see how none of these leads scream at the reader?

These leads are all factual, no empty hype like "I have an incredible offer for you."

Empty hype words like "incredible" and "amazing" are, in fact, the quickest way to ensure your reader stops reading. If you always write with the attitude that your readers are as smart, or smarter, than you are, you will have a far more success.

Get to the point immediately

Has a salesman ever come to your door and stood there talking with you for minutes without saying why he's there?

He asks you how you are doing. He talks about the weather. He comments on how nice your house is and how nice your kids are. You then finally ask, "What are you selling?" . . . if you haven't slammed the door in his face with an "I'm not interested."

The reality is, as soon as your readers open your envelope and see your letter, they instantly know they are being pitched—sold something. And they won't take more than about three seconds to figure out what you've got to sell. They aren't going to read a page or two to find out what your pitch is about.

They'll judge it by the first sentence.

James Bond movies always start with a great action sequence. Never will a James Bond movie start with a long-winded conversation. Opera fans do not go to operas to hear singers clear their throats. They go for the performance.

Your readers want the performance to start with the first sentence.

The power of the word "mistake"

The word "mistake" has the magic quality of making whatever it is you are saying more interesting.

If you say, "Let me tell you about a serious mistake I made that cost me a lot of money," ears will immediately perk up.

Would you rather listen to someone boast about his great achievements? Or would you rather listen to someone talk about his own mistakes as a way to help you avoid making the same mistakes?

People also want to hear about costly mistakes they might be making.

Try incorporating the word "mistake" in your lead sentences and headlines, and see what happens.

Here are a few ideas you might borrow:

- "Have you made any of these investment mistakes?"

- "Don't make this mistake when choosing someone to fix your roof."

- "Would you like to identify and correct the single biggest mistake in your golf swing in just 10 minutes?"

- "Are you among the 90% of parents who make this same mistake when talking to your children?"

- "Here's a mistake I'll bet you're making every day in your marriage."
- "Here's one mistake I hope you never make with your career."

- "Here are the 10 most common mistakes surgeons make in the operating room."

- "I made a big mistake in not writing to you sooner."

- "Let me tell you about the biggest marketing mistake I made that cost me a lot of money and nearly bankrupted me. I don't want you to make the same mistake."

- "I made a serious mistake. I apologize."

People love hearing about mistakes. But using the word "mistake" is especially powerful when talking about your own mistakes.

"For years I was making the same mistakes in my workout and exercise routine. Even though I was going to the gym four times a week, I couldn't figure out why I wasn't getting any stronger. And than I discovered . . ."

You might then follow this introduction with these kinds of questions: "Does this sound familiar? Are you making this same mistake?"

I'm sure you've noticed that the best way to diffuse your customer or client's anger with you is to immediately admit your mistake, followed by an apology. Something along these lines: "I apologize for my mistake. As my way to try to make amends, I have enclosed two tickets for the New York Giants football game."

When a baseball manager apologizes for making a comment that could be interpreted as racist, when he goes on TV and says: "I am truly sorry for my mistake. It was a very stupid choice of words. I did not intend to hurt anyone," people sympathize with the poor fellow who has just been fired from his job. They forgive him if he admits his mistake.

My banker recently made a big mistake with my money. I had asked him to transfer a sizeable sum of money by wire to one of my mailshops. He transferred the wrong amount, adding an extra zero.

Yikes!

The money went out.

When I ran into the bank in a panicked frenzy because my entire bank account had been drained and pointed out the error, the banker made the mistake of trying to blame me for his mistake. He said, "That's what you told me to send . . ." even though the written record of the transaction had the correct amount.

Everyone makes mistakes. I was far less annoyed with his mistake than I was by his effort to try to blame me (the customer!) for his mistake. All he had to say was, "I'm very sorry for my mistake. I'll get the money back into your account immediately."

Talk about a really bad sales tactic!

The word "mistake" has many uses. It's a powerful word to keep in mind for all your marketing and customer relations efforts.

The word helps establish your credibility and trustworthiness. It's an almost magic word that automatically makes whatever you're saying worth listening to.

You can't sell by boring your reader

Fascinating facts, shocking details, riveting narratives keep people listening and reading.

People aren't going to watch a boring movie or finish reading a boring book. The easiest thing for any reader to do is to stop reading and to go on to something else.

Facts and statistics leave everyone cold. What people want is flesh and blood—human stories. *People* magazine, *National Inquirer,* and *Star* are popular publications because they report gossip on famous people. People are interested in people.

In your opinion, which of the following is the better way to communicate your point?

```
"350,000 people die of cancer every year."
```

Or ...

```
"I'm sending you a photo of my little
eight-year-old friend, Jimmy, who died from
cancer today."
```

Reciting statistics and numbers is death in direct mail sales copy. Statistics are impersonal. It's one thing to say six million Jews died in the Holocaust. It's quite another to watch "Schindler's List," read the *Diary of Anne Frank,* or visit the Holocaust Museum in Washington, D.C., where you will see, hear, read, and feel the stories of actual people.

Statistics leave no impression on the brain. Statistics leave the reader uninvolved.

Now you may want to include a few statistics in your direct mail letter to back up some of your claims. And sometimes statistics can be interesting if they are shocking or surprising. But usually not.

Your letter certainly does need to appeal to the brain part of your reader, not just to triggering emotions. But statistics and numbers will not move your reader to buy . . . or even to read further. A stunning story about a real person will. The right story about an actual person will pull your reader into your presentation.

Copy aimed at the heart will always out-pull copy aimed at the mind. Jesus knew this. He used parables, stories that made his points. He did not approach us with data. He did not say 3,000,000 people went to Hell today—though that statement might certainly have gotten the riveted and focused attention of his audience. Remember, your goal is not to win a debate with your reader. Your goal is to move the emotion or impulse side of the brain in such a way that they will buy.

But if you feel you absolutely must use a statistic in your letter to show the magnitude of the problem, try something like this:

> Imagine if the September 11 attack on America happened 100 times a year.
>
> Imagine terrorists flying planes into our buildings, killing 3,000 people twice a week.
>
> But that's exactly what cancer is doing: killing 6,000 people every single week.

This is far more powerful than simply saying, "350,000 people die of cancer every year" . . . because here you are connecting a number to an actual event you know your reader has experienced. You are giving meaning to the number. September 11 was a shocking event for every American. It was an emotional event.

Now you are pointing out that cancer causes just as catastrophic an event more than 100 times a year, every year. By connecting your pitch to an event like what happened on September 11, a catastrophic event we all experienced, you are providing a graphic visual image of the horrifying carnage cancer leaves in its wake each day. You are tapping into your reader's emotions. You are getting your reader involved, in a personal way, to show the magnitude of the crisis you are writing about.

You can then go into your program for how your reader can avoid this catastrophe in her life.

The all-important P.S.

After your reader has read the first line of your letter, the next place she'll likely look is the P.S.

In fact, many people read the P.S. first, because they know that's where they will find the bottom line of why you're writing to them.

The P.S. summarizes the action you want your reader to take and re-states the offer. Try not to simply repeat lines from the letter, but don't depart from your theme either. Keep the P.S. focused and on point.

Remind the reader of the need for the immediate arrival of the check, order, or reservation. I always include a deadline date for the order and explain the reason for the deadline.

The P.S. should also remind the reader about the money-back guarantee. The P.S. is a great place to offer your reader instant gratification by providing a toll-free 1.800 number and online order options so your reader can order immediately and perhaps have the product delivered overnight.

Force an answer

Do everything in your creative power to force your reader to respond in some way.

Ask your reader to send back an answer to your letter — "Yes" or "No."

Asking for a response one way or the other requires the reader to make a decision. You want to give your reader reasons to answer now — to make a decision.

The worst answer for a salesman is "I'll think about it and get back to you later." That means the answer is "no."

But the prospect is also keeping his options open. The easiest answer for your prospect to give is "maybe."

By requiring a "yes" or "no" answer on the spot, you are forcing your prospect to face a moment of truth. "If I answer no, I'll miss this opportunity forever" is the thought you must create in the mind of the prospect. The last thing you want your prospect to think is, "There's no hurry. There's no need for me to make a decision right now."

I've seen women take exactly this approach with men. "You either ask me to marry you now, or that's it. No more waiting. Tonight we will go out to dinner. If I don't have a ring on my finger by the end of dessert, I'm gone. Finito. You'll never see me again."

"Yikes!" the guy thinks. "I guess she's not going to let me string her along for another eight years. I better rush out and get that ring."

A weak salesman does not like forcing this moment of truth, or requiring a "yes" or "no" answer on the spot. A weak salesman believes that if he does not get a "no" answer, he still has a chance to make the sale later.

Wrong. He has very little chance of making any sales with this approach . . . because most people would rather never commit until they absolutely must. A strong salesman knows that forcing a moment of truth and requiring a decision on the spot will certainly produce more definitive "no" answers. But he will also force many more "yes" answers—many more sales.

There are many methods of forcing a decision. You might say in the P.S. "If you decide not to subscribe, would you mind writing me a note telling me why?" Or, "If you decide not to subscribe, please just write 'I am not subscribing' across the order form and mail it back to me. That way I will know you received and read my letter, and I won't bother you again."

I'm sure you've seen the "Yes" and "No" sticker on offers that come through the mail. The marketer here is trying to force you to make "yes" or "no" decision.

I'm not a big fan of these stickers. They don't look like a real moment of truth to me. But that's the effect these marketers are attempting to create in the minds of their readers.

In a fundraising solicitation I mailed, I asked supporters of the organization to return the booklet of "Monthly Gift coupons" and the accompanying "set of 12 reply envelopes" if they had decided not to participate in the monthly giving program I was promoting.

Many of those who elected to return the booklets included a one-time gift. Many of those who returned the booklets were too embarrassed to do so with no gift at all.

So in all your mailings and sales presentations, always think of ways to require a response one way or the other—to force a decision.

Why long letters usually work best?

Testing shows that long letters usually work better than short letters. This is yet another example of how direct marketing is "counter-intuitive."

Common sense would seem to dictate that short letters and short presentations would work better. Who has time to read a four-page or eight-page letter?

But all testing shows otherwise. Long works far better than short 85 percent of the time. A four-page letter will work better than a two-page letter. An eight-page letter will work better than a four-page letter.

This is a general rule. There are, of course, exceptions.

The reason is this: About half the people who answer your letter with an order will have read every word. The other half who answer will have scanned your materials. The scanners read the first line, the P.S., and the reply form, your headlines, and perhaps some of your underlined phrases. And they will review the guarantee. Your scanners don't need a long letter.

But about half your buyers want all the information before they make a decision to buy. These people can't get enough information. And if you fail to answer all their questions, they won't buy. You must write for both audiences: Your scanners as well as those who want all the information.

Of course, there comes a point of diminishing returns. A 16-page letter is overkill in most cases, and may drive your cost up too high, though I have written a number of very successful 16-page letters. The fact that it's 16 pages is enough to get a reader's attention, and suggests that the writer must have a lot of important things to say.

Generally, a 16-page letter will out-pull an eight-page letter, but not enough to make up for the increased cost.

But there are important exceptions to this rule. Subscription and membership renewal notices should be short and look more like invoices than letters. A one- or two-page letter works best here and also keeps your cost lower.

If the service, product, or cause does not need much explaining, a short letter will work best. A dentist might send you a reminder that it's been more than six months since your last check-up. No need, in this case, for this notice to include a long letter describing all his services.

If the President of the United States is writing to his supporters asking for contributions for his reelection campaign, he does not need a long letter. The need is obvious. It does not require explaining. Everyone knows who the President of the United States is. Everyone knows political campaigns cost money. Besides, a Presidential election is in the news everyday. In a case like this, a long letter will be a distraction and will likely depress returns.

Credit card offers are usually short. Everyone knows what a credit card is for. All that needs to be explained is the offer. What is the interest rate? What is the annual fee? What are some of the incentives and benefits? This job can be done on one or two pages.

Long letters will almost always work best in prospecting. Since, in a prospect letter, you are writing to people who have never bought anything from you and who know nothing about you, more explaining will be needed to persuade your reader to try your service.

Your letters to those who have already bought something from you can be a mix of long and short letters, whatever is appropriate. The length of your letter should be determined by how much you have to say. The rule is to answer all the questions your reader might have. If this requires eight pages, write eight pages; if it requires four, write four.

Don't waste words. Make your message simple and compelling. Don't bore your reader. Pull the reader through the copy. The easiest step a reader can take is to stop reading and go on to something else. Your reader will know if you're not saying anything of much importance.

Every word should count. Every word, every phrase, every sentence should have a purpose. All superfluous words and sentences should be ruthlessly cut. But don't cut copy just to make your letter fit on two pages or four pages either. Tell the whole story.

But there's another side benefit of the long letter. A very long letter, eight pages or more, is attention-getting in itself. It adds weight and heft to your package. Kind of makes your #10 envelope, stuffed full of paper, feel like a brick when it arrives in the mailbox. "I wonder what's in here?" your readers will ask themselves.

Don't write an 8- or 12- or 16-page letter just to do it. Make certain you really have enough to say to fill up all this paper. But the attention-getting aspect of a very long letter is a factor to consider. Many of my most successful direct mail packages land with a thud when dropped on the kitchen table.

The longer you hold your reader's attention, the better your odds of getting the sale

The car salesman wants to keep you in the showroom.

He knows that if you leave the showroom, the chance he will ever get the sale is almost nil.

If your reader puts your letter aside, thinking "I'll come back to it later"—you can be near 100 percent certain she will never be back. If she ever comes back, it's a bonus.

On the other hand, if you can write in such a way that captivates your reader (like Stephen King writes), you have a great chance of getting the sale. The longer your prospect reads, the better chance you have of getting the order.

There is only one reason your prospect will continue reading your letter: You are striking a chord with your reader. What you are saying is of intense interest to your reader.

Your reader will continue to read only if it's more difficult for your reader to stop reading than to continue reading . . . because what you are saying is so fascinating.

Order forms and reply forms

The order form is your moment of truth.

Will your reader pick it up and read it? Will she act on your offer?

Make your order form user friendly. Make it as easy as possible to fill out and order your product. The mistake people make in crafting order forms is to require too much information from the reader.

Many order forms I see (both on the Internet and that arrive in the mail) look like they were designed by the legal department or the accounting office, certainly not the marketing people.

Ask for the absolute bare minimum of information you need to process the order. Your order form should not frighten or turn off your reader. It should not look tedious, or be a chore to fill out.

Order forms should look like order forms.

All the information should appear exactly where your reader will expect to find it—not hidden somewhere, not in the fine print. I hate fine print (the product of lawyers) on order forms.

Make sure your customer can easily find out how much to write out a check for and who to write the check to. The money section is the most important section in the package. The money section is of intense interest to your reader. Make the money section easy to find, easy to read, and crystal clear.

A reply form should include a headline that waves a flag at the reader concerning what the offer is about.

The lead sentence, the P.S., and the reply form are the places the reader looks first.

Of those who answer your letter, half will never read the entire letter. They will make their decision to buy based on the first line, the P.S., and what they see on the order form. Reply forms and order forms should contain all the action steps you want your reader to take.

Make it super easy to buy

Make it as easy as possible for your reader to order your product. In all your mailings where you want an order or response of some kind, you should use a postage-paid reply envelope, either a business reply envelope (BRE) or a reply envelope with stamps already affixed.

You never want your reader to put your letter aside because she does not have a stamp readily at hand.

If it makes economic sense, I like affixing actual postage stamps to reply envelopes, rather than using the more customary BRE. Very few people will ever throw away an envelope with live stamps on it, totaling the first class postage amount. To throw this envelope away is like throwing away money, even if the only way you can use these stamps is to mail back this reply envelope—which is exactly what you want your reader to do. But don't just rely on people using the reply envelope to mail in a check with the order form filled out.

Include an option to pay by credit card, by phone, or online. Be sure to include a toll-free 1.800 number and the Web address for an online order form on all major components of your mailing. Be sure your 1.800 number and the URL for your online order form are easy to find.

No matter what component of your package your readers are holding, a way to order easily and instantly should be staring them in the face and prominently displayed.

Keep it simple and clear

The instant your reader is confused by your presentation is the instant she will tune out. Complexity is the enemy of sales.

In fact, complexity is the enemy of communication.

Sell just one thing. Ask for one decision, not many decisions with lots of options. Make your instructions clear, direct, and easy to follow.

> Simple, clear sentences.
> Simple, clear action steps.
> Simple, clear order form.
> Simple, clear headlines.
> Simple, clear reasons.

Chapter Twenty-Two
Letters to business executives

Whether writing to the business executive trying to land the big consulting contract, or selling a newsletter subscription to a consumer, the structures of your arguments are essentially the same.

You still need headlines in your proposal or sales pitch. You still need to construct a "show-and-tell presentation." Business executives are very busy people. Just like the mass-market consumer, if they can't grasp what you are selling, what you are proposing, in about three seconds, you're gone, finito, out the door, never to be seen or heard from again.

The busy, self-important business executive won't give you a second chance—unlike the far more forgiving consumer.

So bore the business executive at your own peril.

But there are clearly some important differences.

If you are selling a high-end product or service to a big successful business, you must come across as highly professional. No offset "Dear Friend" letters here.

You must send business executives letters that look like they are from one person to another—personalized, highly-individualized, business-style letters. Instead of the 50 cents per letter you might spend on consumer offers, you might spend $5 or more on a letter and proposal to a business. Your letter and proposal should arrive with first class postage (not bulk) and perhaps even via FedEx. And the paper you use should be nice bond, perhaps even watermark paper—a quality paper that communicates excellence. Successful business executives want to do business with other successful people. They have no time or patience to meet with a salesman who has holes in his shoes and whose suit doesn't fit.

As in all direct marketing, your presentation must always fit the audience. If you are writing to the chairman of GM, make sure your presentation appears worthy of reading. Make sure it does not look like junk mail. Cut no corners, spare no expense here, because the potential payoff (return on investment) is so big.

And there will be some differences in language. You will need to be more measured in your approach. You will need to sound like a successful executive talking to another successful executive.

But other than these relatively cosmetic differences, the basic structure of your presentation and offer can and should follow the same basic principles. Remember, human nature is a constant. Whether you are rich or poor, you have the same basic motivations. You have fears and frustrations and problems—whether you live in a trailer park or are the Chairman of GM.

Some of the details of your specific problems will certainly be different. But the rich man and the poor man are still worried about basically the same things. They both still worry about money, about legal issues, about the future, about all those sharks circling in the water waiting to devour them, and about all the threats to their well-being that are always out there.

So you still use exactly the same rules of marketing when you are talking with the business executive and the mass-market consumer. You just make sure you change your clothes and adjust your language depending on your audience. You should not talk the same way to long-shoremen as you do to college professors. In all marketing, you must learn and speak the language of those you are talking to.

But the same fundamental principles of marketing always apply.

I once made a decision to try enclosing a $1 bill in a proposal I was sending to a wealthy business executive .

I was urged by my copywriting peers not to do that. "There's just no way a multi-millionaire, a graduate of Harvard business school no less, will respond to a $1 bill package. He will see it as a gimmick and pitch it in the trash."

"Not if I say up front that enclosing this $1 bill is a gimmick," I answered. "Not if we tell our Harvard-educated multimillionaire reader that the purpose of enclosing this $1 bill is to get the attention of a busy executive."

My letter started this way:

Dear Mr. Smith:

I have taken the very usual step of enclosing a $1 bill in a clear plastic envelope for a reason.

I had to think of a way to get your attention for my letter, to make sure my letter stood out from all your other mail.

I would never do something this gimmicky if I were not writing to you about an important matter to you and your company.

But I am a marketing professional. That's how I make my living.

And I have found in more than 19 years of marketing experience that enclosing a $1 bill with my letter, especially if it arrives in a clear plastic envelope, almost always increases response to my sales and marketing letters by 50% or more.

Mr. Smith, I believe I have a number of ways to significantly improve your marketing, perhaps improve your return on investment on all your marketing efforts by 50% or more if you will give me a few minutes of your time.

I would like to come in and meet with you to talk about your marketing.

I have scores of methods and techniques that I use, besides enclosing $1 bills with my letters, that will ensure your letters and your marketing materials are opened and read by your target audience.

In the next few days, I will call your secretary, Linda Johnson, to see if I can meet with you in the next week or two.

> My hope is that you will let Ms. Johnson
> know so she will expect my call. Alterna-
> tively, you may have her call me to schedule
> the appointment.
>
> My direct office number is _____. If she
> can't reach me there, my cell phone number
> is _____.

Guess what happened.

My mailing that included a $1 bill as a gimmick to get the attention of my reader worked even better to the wealthy, highly-educated business executive than to ordinary consumers.

Why? Because, in truth, a wealthy person will pay attention to something interesting just as any mass-market consumer will.

Do wealthy people go to the same movies as regular people?

Yes, they do . . . because they also like to see a good movie. They will also pay attention to a letter that arrives in unusual packaging and will listen to an attractive offer.

But you will also notice with this letter that I invested a great deal of time, effort, and expense in personalization when writing to this wealthy prospect. And I could afford to because the potential payoff was so big.

For example, the letter specifically mentions the name of his secretary. Getting this information requires some individualized legwork. You won't be able to get this information by renting a compiled list from Dun & Bradstreet. You will need to find this kind of personalized information on your own.

The look, feel, and tone of the letter is very important when writing to a business executive. A salesman is far more likely to make a sale to a successful business executive if the clothes of the salesman and style of speaking look and sound right. The same is true for your letter.

Chapter Twenty-Three
The science of persuasion

The single most persuasive word

Again, **contrary to conventional** advertising wisdom, the most persuasive words in selling are not "free" and "new."

The word "BECAUSE" is far more persuasive.

Why?

BECAUSE this word signals to the reader that you have reasons for making the claims you are asserting . . .

BECAUSE this word instantly lets your reader know that you have facts to back up what you say . . .

BECAUSE this word shows your reader that you have put thought into your letter.

BECAUSE is a great word for building credibility.

The word BECAUSE signals that you have facts to support what you are saying. "Hire me BECAUSE . . ." is so much stronger than just leaving it as "HIRE ME!"

And adding an exclamation mark does not strengthen the argument one bit.

Facts sell. And reasons sell . . . BECAUSE facts and reasons persuade. The word "BECAUSE" tells your reader that the rest of the sentence will be "a reason why" what you claim is true, or a reason why I am asking you to take some action.

Suppose your 10-year-old child made this request: "Mom, can I come home later tonight and miss dinner?"

Your response would not be, "Sure, no problem. Come home whenever you can." It would either be to say "No, absolutely not. Get home right now and start your homework." Or, you might come back with a very skeptical, "Why?"—knowing your answer would still be "No."

Your child would have a far greater chance of getting an immediate "yes" if he asked the same question this way: "Mom, can I come home after dinner tonight BECAUSE I've already finished my homework and BECAUSE Jimmy's mom has invited me to have dinner there with them."

The word BECAUSE is very disarming BECAUSE this word tells you that your child is about to follow his seemingly out-of-the-ordinary request with a set of reasons and facts that can easily be checked out.

You might still answer "NO" after hearing his reasons and facts. You might indeed have a stronger set of facts and reasons for denying his request. But the conversation is now engaged. And your son has a far greater chance of getting a "yes" answer from you . . . all BECAUSE he immediately followed his request with the word "BECAUSE."

The #1 mistake
made by writers of sales letters

Facts, reasons, logical arguments, fascinating details, and a great story all help you sell.

The fastest way to guarantee your letter is thrown in the trash is to use the typical empty hype-words amateur writers use all the time in their sales letters.

You know these words well—words like "amazing," "incredible," "awesome," the "best ever," "colossal," and the "greatest."

With compelling facts, reasons, and a good story to tell, there's no reason to use these kinds of meaningless hype words. But these hype words are used so often that not only are they not attention-getting in the least, they have actually become trigger words that cause a reflex action in readers to stop reading immediately.

Most amateur writers of sales letters think raising the volume and screaming at the reader is the best way to make sure the reader listens—when actually it's the surest way to cause your prospect to tune out.

Good copywriting does not imitate the approach of street corner huckster.

The best salesmen are those who have a knack for selling without their customers even realizing they are being sold. The instant your prospect sees that she is being sold, the truth detector machinery in the brain kicks onto full alert and your reader becomes a super skeptic.

Who are you more likely to hire to do a job?

The fellow who is trying to sell you hard, the fellow who seems desperate for work? Or the fellow who does not need the job because he has plenty of business already, the fellow who must clear a spot in his schedule for you because his services are in such demand?

When Stephen King writes, does he use a lot of hype to generate reader interest? Does he scream at the reader? Does he say, "Okay reader, now get ready for the scary part, because this is going to be really, really scary"?

No, he simply tells the story. Readers are pulled along by the fascinating details, the mystery, the intrigue, the suspense, and the storyline. This is how Stephen King gets people to stay up all night reading one of his 600-page books.

Great writers know how to hold the attention of readers without the empty hype. Study Stephen King and how he holds your attention. You will then write much better letters.

Remember, Stephen King is a salesman too. He sells books for a living, and he's sold a lot of them. But it does not matter one bit to his customers that Stephen King is selling them books, because we are completely immersed in the story he's telling, and the fascinating details. We want him to keep writing books . . . so we can buy more.

The most important rule in sales

Obviously, we need to be completely honest and candid in all our business and financial dealings simply as a moral imperative, even if honesty did not work. That should go without saying.

But that's not why I'm saying, "Scrupulous honesty is the most important rule in all sales."

The great news for marketers is that honesty is one of the most powerful and effective sales tools.

The reason is: the American people have become experts at immediately detecting scams and false claims because they have now seen so many. An exaggeration, a claim that seems the least bit suspect, will cause your readers to dismiss everything else you have to say.

In fact, they will just stop reading as soon as they sense they are targets of a snow job.

That's why I am sure in my sales letters to clearly state, even highlight, my weaknesses and shortcomings right up front.

Why do I do this?

Well, for one thing it's probably readily apparent to anyone who meets me what my strengths and weaknesses are. It would be a completely futile exercise to try to present myself as something different than what I am.

Another reason to admit your weaknesses up front in any sales presentation, is that it establishes your credibility. It's disarming. You will immediately see your listeners' guard come down.

And then I will turn my readily admitted weaknesses into strengths.

For example, I usually tell audiences of aspiring entrepreneurs that "I can't hold down an office job in a big company for long, which is why I had no choice but to go into business for myself."

Who would ever admit such a thing?

The audience's ears immediately perk up. They want to hear more. After that shocking admission, I then say something like . . .

> The truth is, most successful entrepreneurs would be fired instantly from most jobs at big established companies . . . because they like doing things their own way. They don't have much patience for bureaucracy and meetings. They are men and women of action. They don't wait for orders from headquarters. They hear the gunfire and ride to the sound of the guns. They don't wait for the committee to decide what needs to be done. When the entrepreneur sees a problem, he tackles it, instantly.
>
> The entrepreneur is not worried about covering his rear end. He just wants to get the job done, and done now. Unfortunately, this is not a personality that is appreciated in most large corporate bureaucracies. Corporate bureaucracies can't act quickly, which is why they always hire consultants like me to do what needs to be done . . . because I can be easily fired. And I don't mind one bit. As a consultant, especially as a marketing consultant, my entire job is to solve a marketing problem and then get fired and move on to solve someone else's marketing problem.

Admitting your weaknesses up front makes everything else you have to say more believable. Admitting your weaknesses and shortcomings also helps define who you are and what you do, why you are different from your competitors . . . who will never admit their weaknesses.

We're not big, established, famous, and prestigious. But because we're small and new, we're more flexible; we'll work harder for your business; your hard-earned dollar will go a lot further with us; we'll care more about you; and your account won't be handled by an inexperienced junior account manager. You'll be dealing everyday with the head of this company, who has more than 19 years experience in this industry.

Avis deployed this ad strategy brilliantly against Hertz, which is the bigger car rental company. Avis admitted in its ad campaign that, "We're #2, so we'll try harder."

What an endearing ad campaign. Plus, Americans love an underdog. Avis is unlikely ever to pass Hertz as the biggest car rental company. But being #2 isn't bad. Most of us would take it.

So, not only is honesty a moral imperative; it's an extremely effective sales strategy.

Think of this truth this way.

Your customers and clients are not idiots. They are intelligent people who hear sales pitches all the time. They know when they are being conned. When a salesman walks into their office or when a direct mail pitch arrives in the mail, their immediate reaction is to get rid of the salesman as quickly as possible and to pitch the direct mail piece in the trash. That's always your potential customer's first impulse.

But obvious honesty and candor where you admit weakness instantly diffuses skepticism. The skeptic's antennae start to go down. Your prospective customer starts to like you and believe what you have to say — that is, until you make a claim that appears to be hype.

The surest path to success in marketing and in business

Focus on helping other people achieve success.

The only way to persuade someone to buy is to offer what she needs or what he is looking for. It's not about what you want. Success in business and in sales lies in figuring out what others want and how to solve other people's problems.

One reason I love marketing, sales, and business generally is that I am always forced to walk in the shoes of others—to put myself in their place when crafting my sales letters and presentations.

I have to figure out, "What can I do to solve their problem? How can I help them? How can I be of true service? How can I be a godsend to them?"

Businesses fail because they focus on their own needs, their own goals, their own wants, their own timetables . . . instead of on what their customer wants.

So be a problem solver. More on point, be a solver of other people's problems.

If you focus on helping others, most of your problems will fix themselves along the way.

Forgetting this seemingly obvious principle is the #1 reason for failure in marketing, in business, and in life.

Raise the level of your guarantee

It's no longer sufficient simply to include a money-back guarantee with your offers. There is nothing remarkable about a money-back guarantee, since all marketers include it.

Dullsville.

The challenge is showing your reader that your guarantee means something, that it's real. This reminds me of the Chris Farley line from the movie "Tommy Boy": "Look, if you want me to take **a** dump in a box and mark it guaranteed, I will."

That's about how much credence your readers place in the word "guaranteed" today.

How do you make your guarantee mean something? How do you make your readers pay attention to your guarantee?

What's required today is a super-charged guarantee—a guarantee, frankly, that requires brass balls (if you're a guy).

Nordstrom's guarantee is one of the most famous.

Nordstrom promises that you can return a Nordstrom product anytime and get a full refund, no matter how long you've had it, no matter how much you've worn it.

There's a story (probably an urban legend) about a guy who brought in a set of tires to Nordstrom, asking for a refund. Nordstrom gave the refund even though Nordstrom has never sold tires. Though this story is probably myth, the fact that this story is so well known just underscores the legendary fame the Nordstrom guarantee has achieved.

Everyone knows about the Nordstrom eye-popping guarantee. The Nordstrom guarantee is so famous that it's now part of the Nordstrom brand. This extraordinary guarantee is what people think of when they think of Nordstrom.

The Nordstrom guarantee communicates far more than just that the purchase is "risk-free" to the customer. This super-charged guarantee communicates that Nordstrom has confidence in the quality of its merchandise, and also that Nordstrom trusts its customers to treat Nordstrom fairly. A relationship of trust is established.

Nordstrom is telling customers that the store is staking its entire business on the quality of its products and on customer satisfaction. In a sense, Nordstrom has built its business and reputation on the attention-getting strength of its guarantee.

And what a brilliant marketing strategy this is, because without this memorable guarantee, Nordstrom would not stand out in people's minds as any different from Nieman Marcus, Bloomingdale's, Macy's, Fields, Saks Fifth Avenue, or a dozen other department stores that offer the same merchandise. The stunning Nordstrom guarantee is what makes Nordstrom different.

I know an accountant who promises his customers that if they ever feel he has failed to save them at least double the cost of his fee on their income taxes versus what they would have paid if they had done their own taxes, he will refund his entire fee.

This accountant has no shortage of clients. As far as I know, he has never been asked for a refund.

One of the biggest challenges we sales letter writers have is to get our readers to read our entire letter—to hear the entire pitch. One way to generate interest in your letter is to build your letter around a stunning guarantee that might read like this:

<u>This Letter Is Guaranteed</u>

You might wonder: "How can a letter be guaranteed?" It's free anyway!

I don't believe this guarantee has ever been made before. So here's how it works:

If you read my entire letter and if you feel, at the end, that it's been a waste of your time, just let me know by writing a note on the back of this certificate and I will send you $20, or donate $40 to the Salvation Army, whichever you prefer.

I am making this guarantee because I know you are very busy running your dry cleaning business.

I also know that I am asking you to take a few minutes of your valuable time to consider what the program I've outlined here can do to help improve the marketing of your dry cleaning business.

Since I'm sending out about 400 of these invitations, this potentially puts me at risk for having to pay out $16,000. But I'm not overly concerned because I'm confident you'll agree that my letter was well worth reading, and because I trust that you have integrity and honor.

I also know that you are a fellow entrepreneur who almost certainly wants to improve the marketing side of your business.

Sincerely,

Ben Hart

Sure, there will be a few jokers out there who will request the $20. But most people (98 percent or more) truly are people of honor and integrity. Nordstrom would have gone out of business long ago if the average consumer had any interest in cheating the store.

Contrary to the impression we might have from the nightly newscasts, the wonderful truth is that the vast majority of people are decent honest hardworking folks who won't take advantage of you and won't try to cash in on your super-charged guarantee . . . unless you really are putting out a shoddy product.

Chapter Twenty-Four

The most important word in direct marketing

The word is "TEST."

Direct marketing is not about conjecture. Nor is it about being creative, original, or finding new frontiers and "going where no man has gone before."

Direct mail marketing is a science developed largely through trial and error. We know what we know mostly because of our past successes and failures. And much of what has proven true in direct marketing we could not have guessed.

Who would have thought long letters would work better than short letters most of the time?

We know because of the results of head-to-head tests. We also know that long letters do not work best all the time.

How do we know? By the results of tests.

We know surveys can work, sweepstakes contests can work, and that membership offers can work (depending on the situation) . . . all because of tests.

How can we know how much to charge for our product until we test different prices? How can we possibly know what combination of incentives in our offer will produce the most orders without test results?

Will our prospect respond better to free frequent flier miles for using our credit card, or "cash back rewards"?

We can't know without test results.

We can make educated guesses. We can have theories. But there's only one way we know if our guesses are right or wrong: TEST.

Without test results, without data, we are flying blind.

Testing will humble even the most expert direct marketers.

Usually a large 9" x 12" carrier will generate more orders than a smaller standard #10, but not always. Usually a personalized letter will produce a bigger response than an off-set, non-personalized "Dear Friend" letter, but not always.

Contrary to what you might have guessed, including a pretty, four-color glossy brochure with your letter will usually depress your returns, but not always.

Sometimes postage-paid Business Reply Envelopes (Bras) work better than reply envelopes that require readers to affix their own stamp, but certainly not always.

In a recent mailing, I was sure putting stamps on the reply envelope would be far more impressive and produce bigger returns than a less personal-looking commercial standard BRE reply envelope you see in junk mail everyday.

A head-to-head test proved otherwise. But this could, and likely will, change for another mailing and another offer to different lists.

Test different headlines. Test formats. Test mailing first class versus mailing at the bulk rate. Test a variety of offers and combinations of offers. Test colors and fonts. Test arguments and reasons.

The most important tests are tests of lists and list segments.

With every mailing you conduct, you should take the opportunity to test something. You only need about 50 replies for a test to be statistically valid. So if you expect a response rate of 2 percent, this would require mailing a test sample of 2,500 names. The larger the test sample, the more statistical validity it has. But even small tests will usually give you the answer to your question.

After more than 19 years in this business I continue to be surprised by the results of tests.

Never assume anything.

When you think about it, there really is no excuse to have a financial disaster in direct mail marketing, because you would never invest in a large mailing until you have test results.

If TEST is the most important word in direct marketing, "ASSUME" is the most dangerous word.

ASSUME is a word that leads to financial ruin.

Chapter Twenty-Five
Narrow is the gate to paradise

The easiest way to make money is to have no competitors.

That's so obvious it's hardly worth stating.

The easiest way to improve your chances of having no competitor, or very few competitors, is to identify a small market niche that you can dominate. It's better to be a big fish in a small pond than a small, struggling fish in a big pond. In the big pond, you will likely be eaten alive very quickly.

In a small pond, you will live a very happy, nearly stress-free, comfortable life.

Let's look again at my very first enterprise, the *Dartmouth Review*. This small conservative renegade and independent student paper was the only source of reporting and commentary on events at Dartmouth written and produced entirely by students. Talk about a refined and narrow product!

So not only was the *Dartmouth Review* different, it had staked out a monopoly. The truth is, the *Review* could have raised $500,000 a year, $1,000,000 a year, or even $10,000,000 a year.

There was almost no limit to the amount of money we, as mere students, could have brought in if we had run the paper like a business instead of as a part-time hobby.

But we were just students. We did not need more than about $150,000 or $200,000 a year to publish the paper and have some money left over for parties. So we just stopped there, sending out a fundraising letter whenever we ran out of money, about four times a year.

So when you think about your product and marketing strategy, think of ways you can give your customers something they can't get anywhere else. And it's best if your market is small and highly specialized, because then the big boys are not as likely to come in and crush you.

Highly specialized information for a niche audience is always great, especially if your niche audience is relatively easy to find. The more specialized, the smaller your potential audience—but also the more committed your audience, and the more you can charge for your newsletter or magazine.

A newsletter with just one editor can do well with 1,000 or even a few hundred subscribers . . . if the cost of a subscription is $95 a month. SEMICONDUCTOR NEWS would be a good candidate for such a business model, or maybe get even more specialized than that. Maybe your publication would do best by focusing on a specific kind of semiconductor. Of course, it's critically important for the information to be really good, essential insider news that semiconductor manufacturers and developers cannot get anywhere else.

The big mistake businesses make is to try to be all things to all people.

For example, the temptation for the editor and publisher of our hypothetical *Semiconductor News* will always be to expand the reach of the publication—to cover the entire high-tech industry. The assumption here is that *Semiconductor News* will reach a wider audience and gain more readers if it becomes *High-Tech News*.

But then the publication is no longer unique. The publication is no longer as valuable to anyone. Your marketing costs will skyrocket as you try to reach this wider audience, and you will have to drop your subscription price radically to have any chance to gain readers, because you will be competing with dozens of other generalist magazines covering the high-tech industry. You will have become a commodity, always competing on price.

Time magazine can never charge much for a subscription because it's a general news magazine. It wants to be all things to all people. As a result, gaining a single subscriber is a Herculean task for *Time* and enormously costly. It takes *Time* about two years on average to pay for acquiring a new subscriber—that is, for the revenue generated by the new subscriber to cover the acquisition cost of that subscriber.

Not many enterprises, especially start-up enterprises, can afford *Time*'s business model. In fact, *Time* is having difficulty affording *Time*'s business model.

Who makes more money in medicine, the general practitioner (who knows something about every health problem) or the neurosurgeon?

The specialist will always earn more.

Narrow is the gate to paradise in marketing.

When you think about it, the path to wealth is not to become bigger, it's to become smaller. The smaller the audience and narrower the focus, the better off most of us will be.

My brother Matt had a rock band. It was pretty good. Very good, actually. Matt is a terrific musician.

The band was getting a solid following in San Francisco. He then decided to take his band nationwide. I advised Matt not to try that. Become big in San Francisco. Maybe just become big in your neighborhood, a subset of San Francisco. If you're good, and I mean really great, you'll break out of your neighborhood when the time is right, when you have a big enough following, and when you have enough cash in your pocket. He did not listen, of course. The band launched its nationwide tour, mostly doing warm-up acts for other bigger-name bands. Everything that could go wrong went wrong, just like in the movie "Spinal Tap." They ran out of money. Their bus broke down. Arguments broke out. Band members quit. Soon there was no band.

The lesson here: Become big in your own neighborhood before you go nationwide. Remember, McDonald's started as just one restaurant serving one neighborhood. Find your niche, become master of your small pond. Because unless you have a billion-dollar marketing budget, you will almost certainly be eaten alive in the ocean.

Chapter Twenty-Six

How to find the money in your customer list

The #1 business blunder

I am stunned and amazed at how few businesses pay much attention at all to their existing customers—those who have actually bought something.

Some businesses don't even keep a customer list!

But it's the first sale that's the toughest. It's much easier to make a sale to someone who has bought from you before than to someone who has never bought from you, might never have heard of you. The reasons are many and should be obvious.

Your customers bought from you because they like what you are selling. They want what you are selling. They need what you are selling. Your customers would much rather continue to do business and buy from someone they know. They would prefer not to buy from a stranger. If your product is any good, selling your customers more of what you know they like should be like shooting fish in a barrel.

For these reasons, it's far more costly to find a new customer than to keep an old one.

Your customers should be hearing from you all the time: a postal mailing once a month, an email communication at least once a week. And not every communication should be a sales pitch. Just give your customers a steady stream of valuable useful information. If you're selling tires, send your customers tips on how to stay safe on the road by rotating tires, maintaining the correct air pressure, and how to measure the tread. Send objective information on what makes a safe tire.

With your communications, your goal is to build a relationship with your customers . . . because when you have a trusted relationship, you have no competition. You will have customers who will faithfully buy from you.

Mining your customer list

You know about the "80/20 Rule." I touched on it earlier, but it's such an important concept that I'll expand and explain it in more detail. The 80/20 Rule is part of Marketing 101. The rule is this:

- 80% of sales come from 20% of customers.

- 80% of commissions are earned by 20% of salespeople.

- 80% of the wealth in America is produced by 20% of the people.

- 80% of sales are generated by 20% of the businesses.

- 80% of your income is produced by 20% of your activities.

- 80% of your revenue is generated by 20% of your clients.

- 80% of donations are made by 20% of the donors.

The reason for this is fairly obvious.

If you observe human behavior, you'll immediately notice that about 20 percent of the population is pulling the wagon—that is, doing about 80 percent of the work and generating 80 percent of the wealth.

Everyone else is riding the wagon, hoping someone else will pull them along.

The great majority of people don't have the guts or energy to start their own business. Most people would rather ride along on someone else's wagon, happy enough in their 9-to-5 job and collecting a regular paycheck every month, while doing as little as possible to earn it.

In the charitable arena, the rule is the same. About 20 percent of the population are givers. The rest of the population are takers.

Actually, the "80/20 Rule" is more like the "90/10 Rule" if we were to really analyze the facts carefully.

But if you were to break down the population even more precisely, you would see that the top 10 percent are the true producers and givers— the true wagon-pullers. There's a middle 60 percent who are happy to ride in the wagon most of the time, but will help out once in a while if they are shamed into it. And then there's the bottom 30 percent of the population who must be dragged behind the wagon in the dirt. These are dead weight who actually hinder progress.

So now let's rename our rule of life the 30/60/10 Rule.

- 30% are dead weight you are pulling along in the dirt.

- 60% are riding in the wagon, not doing much, but not hindering your progress either.

- 10% are doing 90% of the pulling.

The #1 mistake businesses make is to focus too little attention on the 10 percent of customers who are providing 90 percent of your income — and too much attention on the rest who aren't profitable for you at all and, most likely, are costing you money.

The tendency is to take your best customers for granted. "We don't have to worry about these customers because they love us already," is the thought process at work here. We get lazy with these customers because we know these customers are profitable. We then invest enormous effort and resources to try to make our money-losing customers profitable. We continue to send these money-losers newsletters and mailings. We continue to coax, cajole, and bribe in the hope that these people will, someday, become interested in what we are doing.

We make the dead-weight money-losers the focus of our marketing.

What a catastrophic mistake this is!

One of the quickest, easiest ways to increase your profitability is immediately to cut loose the 30 percent of the dead weight, the people (customers and employees) who are costing you money, and will never be profitable no matter what you do. Just get rid of them and at least make your wagon lighter to pull.

Your next step is to give your top 10 percent or 20 percent a lot more tender loving care and to offer more and more of whatever it is that makes these gold-plated customers love you so much. If they like milkshakes, keep offering them bigger and bigger milkshakes. Don't think, "He's already had his milkshake for the month, so no need to offer another milkshake until next month." Keep feeding your gold-plated top 10 percent of your customers more and more of what you know they love. And treat them as the dear and loyal friends they are to you and your business—because you can't survive and prosper without them.

Why is it that most of us are so obsessed with trying to win over the bottom 30 percent?

Why is it that we are more concerned with trying to turn the dead weight we're dragging along in the dirt into wagon-pullers?

I think it's because entrepreneurs are also evangelists at heart. We are so excited about whatever it is we are doing and the service we are offering that we just can't believe most people could not care less about what we are doing. We try to win them over. We are preachers who want as many people in church as we can get. We try to convert these people to the faith. We try even harder to win back our "lost sheep"—our former customers who left us. We just can't believe they left us even after all the great service we provided. It's depressing to lose a customer. Rejection is always depressing. So we spend a lot of money and effort trying to get these "lost sheep" and "prodigal children" back into the fold.

The reality is you will never turn a wagon-rider into a wagon-puller. And you will never turn dead weight into wagon-riders, much less into wagon-pullers. We are genetically wired to be who we are. We were that way at birth.

You are far better off cutting loose the dead weight immediately. In fact, you would be better off getting rid of most of your wagon riders. They aren't much good to you either. Keep a few of the wagon riders around who show some potential of being wagon-pullers. And then focus 80 percent of your efforts on your top 20 percent—your very best customers and clients.

Of course, you will always need to prospect for more customers. You always need to find new prospects to pour into the top of your marketing funnel.

But you must do this knowing that only 20 percent (or less) of your new customers will ever be worth much to your business.

Can you see how clearly understanding this principle can affect, even dramatically change your marketing approach—might even change your business model?

With this principle in mind, your job is not to work to turn your dead weight and wagon-riders into wagon-pullers for you, but to develop a system that will identify your wagon-pullers as quickly as possible so you can focus your attention on them.

Identify, cultivate, and harvest your wheat. Quickly identify and burn the chaff. And you will vastly increase your profitability.

The enormous value of your "multi-buyers"

Your mailings and marketing to your customers who have bought something more than once from you will be at least three times more productive than to those who have bought something from you only once.

If someone bought some exercise equipment from you, you need to be selling more exercise equipment to that person. I am amazed that so many companies only have one product to offer and have only mailed one offer to their customer list. Some businesses actually exist entirely off income from prospecting to cold lists, and have never thought of continuing to offer their list of customers more of the same. If someone buys a treadmill from you, come back with an offer for a better treadmill, or a weight machine. If a golfer bought a driver from you, offer a revolutionary new sand wedge or your new "deadeye" putter.

You know this buyer is a golfer. So keep selling him golf stuff.

A mature customer list or "housefile" is far more productive than a new housefile for the simple reason that you have identified your core of multi-buyers—your regular faithful customers.

In addition, you have stopped mailing regular offers and promotions to most of those who have not bought anything for you in 18 or 24 months, which slashes the cost of your marketing. The older your active customer list—assuming you are mailing regularly (every month or more)—the more productive it will be for each letter you mail.

For this reason, I consider the prospect program to have two parts. There's the prospect program to your outside lists, designed to find your first-time buyers. But then there's the prospect program to your housefile that's aimed at persuading your first-time buyers to buy again. In this sense, your multi-buyers are your true housefile, because these are folks who clearly like what they are getting from you and who have made a conscious decision to continue supporting you through their purchases. They have chosen to join your family.

Become part of your customer's regular routine

An iron law of marketing is that people are creatures of habit.

I always buy Crest toothpaste. I don't know why. I just always have, I guess because my mom bought Crest when I was a kid. I know I need toothpaste. I know this toothpaste works. And Crest is well known because of relentless advertising over many decades. It would take some effort to persuade me to switch to another toothpaste.

Other companies are spending billions of dollars to persuade people to use their toothpaste instead of Crest. But they aren't having much impact on me because I'm used to Crest. I'm comfortable with that brand.

People who have chosen to buy your product instead of your competitor's would prefer to stick with you. To switch their allegiance to another comparable product is to admit that they had made a wrong decision—in effect, to admit a failure. It's very difficult to change people's buying patterns, because this means moving people out of their comfort zones.

People are creatures of habit. But you will lose your customers if they lose sight of you—that is, if they stop receiving communications. Or if they receive communications so infrequently that you are no longer a part of their regular routine, no longer a part of their everyday life.

Email makes it very inexpensive to stay in nearly daily contact with your customers.

Your email communications should not all be sales pitches. Very few should be. Your email communications should provide valuable information that you know will be of interest to your customers.

You must constantly put your organization, your business, your service, your product, in front of your supporters—just like Nike, Coca-Cola, McDonald's, and every successful corporation that depends on the average consumer for business. This is such a basic principle of marketing that I am stunned at how few small businesses understand it.

How to reduce requests for refunds

The money-back guarantee is an essential staple of marketing and business. Especially if you are selling a big-ticket item, those who order will be subject to a natural human emotion known as "buyer's remorse."

"Did I really need that?" is a question that people will have. "Have I just been conned? Is this a waste of money? Will this product really do what the letter promises? Did I get a good price? Is this just another scam?"

To mitigate "buyer's remorse," follow-up the order with a letter, an email, and even a phone call aimed at reassuring your customer—who bought from you because she believed what you told her.

I'm sure you've asked these same questions yourself after buying something pricey.

Most refund requests come in right away—seldom weeks or months later. That's because "buyer's remorse" sets in right after the purchase and then fades over time, even if the customer isn't thrilled with your product. It's during those first few days immediately after the purchase that the threat of a refund request is most acute.

So your follow-up campaign after the purchase is very important. It's a critical marketing element ignored by most businesses.

Your letter should congratulate your customer on her purchase. Reassure her that she made the right decision. Your letter should restate the promises you've made and offer to help her if she has any trouble using your product. Encourage her to call you, or her customer service representative, if she's having any difficulty. Stay in communication with your customer to make sure the product is working as anticipated.

By following up like this, you will diffuse any anxieties and frustrations your customer might be having. Most importantly, you will begin to develop a relationship with your new customer that will set the stage for many more sales to this customer in the future.

Managing your customer list

Your customer list is the lifeblood of your business. Your customer list or "house list" is the result of all your marketing efforts. Your house list is your moneymaker.

These people have shown with their orders and purchases that they like what you're selling. Here are some crucial rules and procedures for managing your customer list.

1. Set up a computerized database.

Some organizations do this themselves. Others maintain their database at a professional database maintenance company. If you decide to do this yourself, there are some off-the-shelf computer programs designed specifically to help you set up your own customer list. What you do will depend on the size and complexity of your database.

Setting up and maintaining a large database of buyers and customers can be an enormous, highly technical task that requires software, a data-entry system, and computer technicians who understand marketing.

2. Set up your order taking and data-entry system.

If you are a mail order business, envelopes must be picked up at the post office, opened, checks deposited, and information entered into your database. This is called batching and caging in direct mail jargon. You will also be taking orders over the phone and over the Internet. There are large companies that specialize in taking your orders for you. But if you are a small operation, you might also do this yourself.

The critical point here is that you will need to set up a system for getting all the necessary information (names, postal addresses, email addresses, order amounts, products ordered, number of units orders, and any other pertinent pieces of information) into your computer database. Making sure this information is entered accurately into your database is absolutely critical to the success of your business.

Think of it this way: I might spend $25 (in prospect losses) to find a new $50+ buyer. If the name of the customer is incorrectly spelled by the data entry person, my investment in finding this new customer is greatly diminished, if not completely lost. Certainly my ability to conduct a highly personalized marketing campaign to that person is destroyed. Wrong personalization is worse than no personalization in your letter. Data-entry errors are very costly to your business.

One way I guard against this is to have the name and address entered in the computer twice. If the information is entered exactly the same way both times, we assume it's correct. This is called double data-entry verification.

This procedure might double the price of your data entry but will be well worth the added cost. As an alternative, you might also consider partial double data-entry verification for your low-dollar customers, in which only the name of the buyer and zip code are entered twice. It's most important to get the name exactly right. The post office can usually deliver the mail even if the address is slightly off.

Other steps to cut down on data-entry errors include "finder number" and barcode scanning systems, which I won't get into here. These systems also have their shortcomings.

I'm always looking for ways to cut down on these costly mistakes. Data-entry errors are one of the biggest problems in direct marketing.

3. Collect as much useable information on your customers as you can.

The most important information you'll need to collect is the product ordered, the number of units ordered, the amount paid, the date of the order, the offer that generated the order, and the list the order came from. This will allow you to know what product and offer your customer liked and will allow you to tailor your future offers to what you now know he likes.

You need a coding system to keep track of what offers your customers answered. The codes for each mailing go on the order or reply form.

You should also strive to collect as much personal information as you can on your buyers, especially your best buyers. You might ask for birthdays and the names of their family members as part of a survey. You'll be able to write far more personal appeals if you have this information. You'll dazzle your reader if you're able to ask how members of their family are doing and reference their actual names. Your customers will be amazed if you remember their birthdays and send a birthday card. Obviously, you can't afford this level of personal treatment for someone who has bought a $15 item once. But it's worth knowing this information on someone who's spending $1,000 or more with you every year.

You'll also want to ask for phone numbers, fax numbers, and email addresses. And be sure you know the gender of each customer and their proper title (Mr., Mrs., Ms., Miss, Dr., Father, Reverend, etc.). Gender is important because women and men respond differently to different approaches, even if the product you are selling is gender-neutral. And getting the title right is as important as getting the rest of the name right.

Try to find out what name they use in casual conversation. The name might be James, but the person might go by Jim. You should know the person's familiar name to make your communications more personal.

Each bit of information should be contained in its own separate field on your database so that you can retrieve it piecemeal and as needed. A copywriter must be familiar with all information available on a database to write an effective, highly personal letter that will sound like you know the person. The more information you have on your customers, the more personal you can make your letters.

This will dramatically improve the performance of your mailings and marketing efforts. But make sure the information you're collecting for your database is useable in your letters, for segmenting your list, and for the overall management of your marketing efforts. Have a specific, well-thought-out purpose for every piece of information you are collecting.

I've seen organizations go overboard in collecting data on customers they will never use. This is just a waste of money and makes your database unmanageable.

4. Make sure there aren't duplicate names in your database.

There are few things more annoying to your customers than receiving multiple copies of the same mailing on the same day. Talk about destroying your attempt to make your letter as personal as possible!

Computer programs can identify likely duplicates, but they aren't perfect.

For example, a computer program can identify two records where the name is spelled differently but is at the same address as a likely duplicate. For your best customers, perhaps the best 20 percent of your file, a human eye should examine the records, printed out in alphabetical order, to identify not just possible duplicate records, but other potential problems with the data that only a human eye and brain with the capacity to make judgments will notice.

You should not rely exclusively on a computer program to keep your housefile list clean— especially your top 10 percent or 20 percent of your customers. It's well worth the effort and cost to examine the records of your best customers with human eyes.

5. Steps to keep your housefile list clean and accurate.

Be a fanatic about the hygiene of your housefile list. And I mean a nut case. There are few things more important to the success of your direct mail marketing program.

Running your list through a National Change of Address (NCOA) program at least every six months will help. NCOA is a constantly up-dated database generated by the U.S. Postal Service. About 15 percent of Americans change their address every year, and any list loses about 50 percent of its value every two years if it's not "NCOAed."

Your reply forms should always include an instruction to your reader in red to "Please make any necessary corrections to your name and ad-dress on this reply form." Be sure any corrections your customers write on reply forms are entered into your database.

Verify names and addresses during telemarketing calls, and make sure the changes are made in your database. Undeliverable first class mail will be returned to you by the post office. These are called nixies or pixies in direct mail jargon. Remove the bad addresses after making every effort to correct the bad addresses. You can also print "Address Correction Requested" on your carrier envelopes and, for a fee, the post office will correct a high percentage of wrong addresses. This service can be costly, so do this perhaps only twice a year.

Send out questionnaires periodically to your customers asking them to verify and correct the information you have on them. Questionnaires provide a great opportunity to update and correct errors on your data-base, and also to ask other questions that will help you in your marketing. Consider offering some incentive to your supporters, such as a gift or special report, for every questionnaire completed and returned.

Standardizing formats, merging multiple files, eliminating duplicates, and updating and verifying addresses are all essential to keeping your house list productive. Failure to keep your list clean and accurate can and probably will bankrupt you quickly.

6. Establish your "unduping" policy.

"Undupe" is direct marketing slang that means eliminate duplicates between the lists you are mailing.

I do not want my best customers to receive prospecting letters. I use the computer to "undupe" these names against all prospect lists because I want to treat these people as special. I want to treat these folks like I know them, as friends. I also want to sell these customers higher-end products. I want to up-sell these folks.

But this rule likely only applies to the top 20 percent or 30 percent of the best buyers on your customer list. The rest of your house list (the bottom 70 percent or so) can and should continue to receive prospecting offers—that is, you can treat them as though they are not on your house list. So don't "undupe" these names against prospecting lists.

"House list" is a somewhat elastic term.

For the purpose of this discussion, I define it as those who have bought something from you within the last 12 months. After that, they are treated as prospect names.

The reasons for not "unduping" the bottom 70 or even 80 percent of your house list against the prospect lists you are mailing are many. But here are three key reasons for making sure these weaker buyers are not omitted ("unduped") from your prospect mailings:

1) **You want to identify your repeat buyers as quickly as possible because your multi-buyers are at least three times more likely to buy again than those who have not bought again from you.**

   Many on your house list will respond with a purchase to a prospect package. Some will respond only to prospect offers, and don't care much about personalized offers and don't respond to "up-selling." Buyers are not very valuable to your business until they become repeat buyers.

2) **You know only one thing for certain about customers who have bought just once from you.**

They liked that offer. So do your level best to keep sending them more of the same. If they like Coca-Cola, keep selling them more Coca-Cola. Don't keep trying to sell them chocolate milk if they keep declining this offer.

3) **"Repeat, repeat, repeat" your message is a key marketing principle.**

Nike, McDonald's, Crest, Tide, and the most successful consumer brands show the same ads over and over again because they know it will take many impressions on your brain before their message sinks in. The same is true in direct mail, which is just another form of advertising.

Your message must be simple, focused, and repeated over and over again to your target market. Just because they answered your letter once does not mean they remember answering it. Nor does it mean they could explain to their friends what you do, what your product is, or even tell them the name of your company. Most people answer direct mail offers out of impulse. They liked what they read at that moment. They ordered the product and then went on to something else. A few days later, they've forgotten your letter and your company completely. They probably will forget they even ordered your product until they receive it.

The big advertisers know this fact of life. They know they can't stop repeating their message to their target audience. They know the battle for market share is really a battle for a share of people's attention, a battle for minds. That's why you should continue mailing a successful prospect package until it stops working. It's also why you should not "undupe" your house list against prospect lists, except for the best 20 percent or 30 percent of your customers who clearly do know about you and your company and should be treated with extra care.

I would say there are very few good reasons to prevent the bottom 70 percent of your house list from receiving prospecting letters. In fact, not keeping these names in your prospect mailings can be catastrophic to both your house list and prospecting mail programs.

And the reason is this:

Unduping your entire house list against prospect lists can cut your prospect results in half if you have a large housefile of 100,000 buyers or more. Someone must pay for prospect losses (the continued building of your house list). It might as well be the weaker names on your house list who help pay for your customer-acquisition program.

Unduping your entire house list against prospect lists will also hurt your house list offers by failing to deliver more prospect mail to your one-time buyers, which, in turn, will give them fewer opportunities to become multi-buyers.

Your prospect "customer acquisition letters" are usually your least expensive packages, because they're produced in large quantities. Making sure your weaker customers receive prospect mail is a great way to keep your company's name or your brand name in front of your luke-warm buyers. And you're achieving this goal with low-cost packages that have proven to be successful.

Chapter Twenty-Seven

How to rent lists to prospect for customers

Not enough attention is paid to lists by direct mail marketers.

In fact, I know of no one in my profession who spends enough time on lists—including me.

The list, or list segment, you select for your mailing is far more important than the letter itself.

The list—that is, the qualified prospects you are trying to sell to—is the single most important element of your marketing campaign. It's possible for a poorly written letter to work to a good list. But it's impossible for a fantastic letter to work to the wrong list. The list is not just a way to reach your market. It is your market.

I'll discuss lists for your prospecting program first, and then your program to your customer list—your housefile.

Lists for prospecting

I covered a number of lead generation strategies earlier, so I won't be getting back into them much here. In this section, I will mostly focus on lists you can rent.

The mailing list business is an enormous industry. There are approximately 30,000 lists available for rental. There are about one billion names on these lists.

If you wonder why you receive so much mail every day from businesses, charities, political causes, and candidates all wanting you to send money for something, it's because your name and address is being rented by list owners, list managers, and list brokers. Your name is being rented or sold, most likely because you bought something through the mail or you contributed to some cause in response to a letter.

Once you're on a mailing list, it's very difficult to get off, because your name and address is being sold and rented to dozens of organizations and businesses. You would have to not answer a piece of junk mail for about three years before you would start to see a noticeable decline in the amount of commercial and fundraising mail in your mailbox.

You would also have to not buy anything over the Internet, not use your credit card, not subscribe to any magazines, and not fill out any forms that ask for your contact information at stores. In addition, you would need to move to a poor neighborhood. If you live in a wealthy neighborhood, you'll receive a lot of direct mail just because direct mail marketers know you have money to spend.

What you're looking to rent are lists of folks who have bought the same kind of product you are selling. If you are selling exercise equipment, rent lists of people who have recently bought exercise equipment, because you know these people are interested in fitness. If you are selling gardening products, rent lists of people who regularly buy gardening products.

In the direct mail business you typically do not buy a mailing list. You rent a list for a one-time use. If you want to mail to the list again, you must rent it again. But anyone who answers your letter becomes part of your customer list—or housefile. In other words, the name is now yours and you are free to continue to send letters to that person without renting that name again. But you are not permitted to continue to mail letters to those who do not respond to your prospect appeal unless you rent the list again.

What you want are buyers who have bought a lot of what you are selling—multi-buyers. And you want buyers who have bought something recently, within the last six or 12 months.

You might need to pay more for these premium names, but it will almost always be worth it. I would much rather pay more for names that I know will be good than less for names that I'm unsure of.

The more recent the purchase, the better the prospect.

This is an important point, worth underscoring, because it's counterintuitive. You might think these would be the weakest prospects on the assumption that these buyers might be tapped out since they just bought. But these recent hotline frequent buyers are, by far, the most likely to answer your letter with an order.

Those who have not bought anything, at least as far as you know, for a long time are weak prospects.

Once you build a sizeable customer list, you'll then have some clout to start negotiating name-exchange agreements with marketers who sell similar products, and this can help you save money on list rental fees. A name exchange is when you allow one marketer to mail to your list of buyers in exchange for that organization or business letting you mail to its list of buyers.

A great living can be made by just learning lists. Learn everything about lists.

Attend seminars on lists. Learn all the list jargon and terms, so you don't sound like an amateur when ordering lists. Think about lists all the time. Ask about lists. Subscribe to every direct mail marketing publication, such as **DM News** and **Direct Marketing** magazine, where you will find countless ads from list companies advertising their lists. Become a member of the Direct Marketing Association. And make a special point to attend direct mail marketing seminars, which are offered all the time by the Direct Marketing Association.

Many mailing lists can be found through the Standard Rate and Data Service, which publishes the **SRDS Direct Marketing List Source.**

This service will tell you what lists are available on the open market, describe the list, and tell you who to contact to rent a list. SRDS breaks down lists into many different categories for direct mail business offers and fundraising solicitations.

The Marketing Information Network (MIN) offers more than 20,000 lists online. Dun & Bradstreet compiles lists of businesses and the executives of these businesses. D&B also compiles lists of individuals by profession.

There are many list services and list brokers. You should find a reputable list broker to help you who specializes in the market you are trying to reach.

Be open to hand-compiling your own lists, especially for highly-targeted appeals that hold out promise of a big return on investment, and not just relying on renting lists that are on the open market. Become a list maniac.

The following are some crucial points to keep in mind when conducting your list work for your prospecting program.

1. Be crystal clear in your list orders.

A mistake in the way you order names can be catastrophic. It's very easy to fall into direct mail jargon, and then discover later that different people attach different meanings to the jargon. When ordering a list from a list broker or an organization, write your order very clearly, precisely, and in plain English. Find out what terms they use and exactly what each term means. Get on the phone with the list broker and go over your written list order verbally, line by line, word by word. Assume nothing.

Make sure you understand exactly what kind of names you are getting for your mailing. Get everything in writing. If you're not sure what their terms mean, get clarification IN WRITING.

2. Learn how to read a list data card.

Even if you use a list broker, you will still be making the decisions as to what kinds of names you want to order from particular lists for your mailing.

Learn how to read a list data card. This is jargon that means a sheet of paper that describes a particular list and what segments are available for rent. Each data card includes a paragraph or two about the background of the list and how the list was compiled. You will want to know what percentage of the list is direct mail generated. You will want to know the precise product and service offers that built the list.

Understand the terms and the selects available for rent. In general, the more name selection options available the better. You may be able to select not only according to buying history and date of most recent purchase, but also by frequency of purchase, gender, age, geographic region, and income level.

Pay careful attention to what kinds of businesses and organizations have rented a list you are considering, and especially which ones have rolled out or mailed a continuation with this list. Were their product offers similar to yours?

If so, this is probably a good list to test. If you see a lot of tests but few continuations, this is likely a weak list.

Question every list's hygiene. Ask how often the list is updated and corrected. Many list suppliers will guarantee the cleanliness of their lists and refund postage costs on letters returned (called pixies or nixies) in excess of some reasonable percentage. About 15 percent of the population moves every year, so lists go out of date very quickly. Ask tough questions about the hygiene of lists you're renting. Try hard to get guarantees of list cleanliness in writing.

Another important factor to consider is the direct mail techniques used to build the list you're considering renting. For example, some lists are built mainly on sweepstakes offers, are therefore not likely to be strong prospect lists for a conventional sales appeal. Others are built mostly on front-end free gifts. Ask the list supplier about the kinds of packages that built the list.

And always test before you roll out, especially on a list that you have not used recently. Often lists can appear very similar from their data card descriptions but will yield radically different results. The data card descriptions will guide your initial decision to test a list, along with guidance from the experienced list broker you've hired. But only your test results can dictate whether you continue or roll out on a list.

3. Find a great list broker.

List brokers are a great resource. List brokers are paid on commission. Usually they take a 20 percent commission on names they find and supply for you. This commission is paid by the list owner, not you. You would typically pay the same for a list whether or not you use a list broker—though, as in real estate transactions, this can also be negotiated.

You want to make sure your list broker is paid well, and that your relationship is a profitable one for the broker. Good list brokers are worth their weight in gold.

Be sure you select a list broker who specializes in the market you're trying to reach. If you're selling a newsletter subscription, don't use a list broker who specializes in product catalogues.

But don't rely on your list broker to make decisions. Your list broker only makes recommendations. You and only you will make your final list decisions. So even if you have a list broker, you should still make a habit of collecting and studying List Data Cards.

4. Appeals should be tailored to lists you're mailing.

Most direct mailers mail one-size-fits-all prospect packages. This is especially so when one has found a control package. The "control" package is direct mail jargon for an organization's most successful prospect package. A prospect package is a control package if it's successful and is beating all other prospect packages. When another package proves more successful, it becomes the new control.

But once you have a successful prospect package, make adjustments in the copy to appeal to specific lists and audiences. When you acquire a list, you are gaining access to a market. Each list has its own unique characteristics.

People on a list are united by a particular interest. Your letter should be written to take that interest into account. For example, you might be writing a letter to people who are subscribers to a certain magazine. Reference the magazine in the first few lines of your letter to show you know something about the person to whom you are writing. You'll need to get the list owner's permission to do this.

5. Test various segments of a list.

Often I hear direct mailers say that a list they tested did not work. I then find out that they only conducted one 5,000-name test of 0-to-18-month buyers from the list. Maybe this select from this list doesn't work. But narrowing your select to 0-to-6 month buyers might work just fine. Or maybe the list owner will let you mail to multi-buyers only, which are at least three times stronger than one-time buyers.

You should also conduct gender tests. Women and men respond differently. Some products, even if they are not gender specific products (insurance, for example) might nevertheless appeal more to women or more to men. A list that might not work well if you mail both to men and women might work if you mail your appeal to just women or just men, depending on the product.

Geography can also make a difference. If you are selling Bibles, maybe your offer will work best in "Bible Belt" states. If you are selling gun-related products, maybe you should stick to rural areas, where there are a lot of hunters. Test to find out. You should also test by age and income if possible. The point is to not assume a list is no good for you just because your test of one broad select failed. Be surgical in your testing. Find out every select the list owner will let you test. Choose a series of intelligent tests.

You'll likely have to pay more for detailed and narrow selects, but the bigger return may well be worth the extra cost. And don't just accept what's printed on the data card as the only selects available. Negotiate the selects you want with the list owner. Be a strategist. Come at the prospect list you're renting from many different angles.

6. Repackage successful appeals and re-mail them to the same lists.

Successful packages can often be repackaged with different techniques, carriers, formats, and graphics and re-mailed through prospect lists that have worked well.

People remember how packages look, not so much the specific words that are in a package. By putting otherwise identical packages in different clothes—such as different looking envelopes, different colors, different paper stock, different graphic layout—most of your readers will assume it's a different letter.

As always, however, be sure to test your different looking packages. A change in the way a package looks can dramatically affect returns, up or down. For example, I was using a yellow post-it note very successfully for a prospect appeal I had been mailing for months. I then tried using a light blue post-it note instead, just to change the look and to see if color was important. My returns dropped 25 percent. In this case, keeping the post-it note yellow was important, I guess because it looked more like a standard yellow post-it note people are used to seeing.

So make changes to the look and feel of your successful prospect packages. Constantly experiment. And always test your changes.

7. If you're prospecting with a non-sweepstakes offer, require the list owner to remove all "sweeps-only" buyers.

Some marketers have built a large portion of their house list with sweepstakes offers. An offer that uses a sweepstakes contest to draw the reader into the letter is a powerful marketing technique. But responders to sweepstakes offers tend to answer only offers built around a sweepstakes contest and are weak prospects for conventional marketing packages. It's fine if a buyer has answered both sweepstakes and conventional offers. What you don't want are sweeps-only or unique-sweeps buyers if you're mailing a conventional sales pitch. This little instruction can make an enormous difference in the performance of your prospecting campaign.

Remember, smart direct mailers spend a lot of time weeding out people who are least likely to respond. Sweeps-only buyers are not likely to answer your conventional sales offer. Weed them out.

Chapter Twenty-Eight
Summing up

The difference between true marketing (as I've been describing to you here) and Madison Avenue advertising is this:

Unlike all your letters, emails, and direct response ads, the 60-second advertisements you see on TV promoting the major brands are not aimed at generating immediate sales and inquiries. And they don't. There are no results to measure for the Madison Avenue ad.

These ads are designed to create brand recognition and public awareness. They are aimed at making the public familiar with the brand and the name of the product.

There is no real way to precisely measure the effectiveness of these Madison Avenue ads. The big corporations know they must advertise. And they are just left hoping their ads are successful. But there's no real benchmark for success, other than the decision-makers at the corporation signing off on the big ad buy.

We certainly know these ads are successful for the ad agency, some of which are racking up billions of dollars in billings. But we have no precise way of knowing if these ads are successful for the client . . . because no orders or inquiries are arriving at the office in answer to these ads.

In this sense, the Madison Avenue ad agency's primary mission in life is not to create ads that win customers, but to create ads that impress the corporate client. If the ad happens to be good and brings customers in, that's a bonus for the ad agency. But who will ever know if that's what's happening?

The primary mission of the Madison Avenue ad agency is to sell the client on the ad campaign, not to create ads that actually sell product.

Who really knows how all those Nike ads are doing?

The ads are attention-getting and interesting. They have certainly done a great job of creating brand awareness and a hip image for the company. I certainly enjoy the Nike ads. No doubt the ads are doing well for Nike and are helping Nike build its image around the world. But Nike has no way of knowing how each individual ad is doing. Nike has no idea how many sales each individual ad is generating. Nike really has no way of knowing its "return on investment" for each ad launched.

The best Nike can do is guess. The best Nike can do is ASSUME its ads are effective.

But even if Nike's "building brand awareness" and image advertising method is working well for Nike (and I'm sure it is), there's very little any of us can learn from this approach. There's no model here for the entrepreneur to follow.

"Go out and just copy Nike" would be silly advice for you because you don't have a multi-billion dollar advertising budget.

It would cost you hundreds of millions, more likely billions, of dollars in advertising to create an image and a "general public awareness" of you, your company, your brand, or your product.

Then you would need to have in place a massive manufacturing infrastructure and a nationwide distribution network to make sure your product is available everywhere.

It would be enormously costly for you to follow the Nike "build brand awareness" and image strategy even in the smallest of local markets. The production of these TV ads alone is a major undertaking.

This big corporate approach is of zero use to you or me. If it were useful, you would not have gotten this far in this book.

The other approach is to sell people our products and services in one-on-one personal conversations.

That's what salesmen do. This is how the rest of us, who don't have a billion-dollar advertising budget, must make our living.

But since the salesman cannot be everywhere all at once making his one-on-one presentations to prospective customers, the next best thing are the systems I've described here.

I believe the most powerful of all marketing tools is the sales letter. The sales letter, for much less cost than a personal one-on-one meeting, seeks to start a conversation with your prospect with the aim of selling your product or service.

Sometimes you can sell the product on the strength of the letter alone. Sometimes, for high-priced products and services, you just want to find out if there's interest in what you are selling—that is, you are seeking to generate qualified leads. Either way, the goal of your mailing is clear and the results are precisely measurable.

The Internet and direct response space ads and radio ads are also wonderful tools if used properly.

Everything you do must be direct response. Remember, if your marketing is not exactly and precisely measurable, it's really not marketing, it's PR.

The Madison Avenue ads are PR. This book is about true marketing—that is, showing you how to produce results that are precisely measurable.

That's the difference between the sales letter or lead generation letter and the image advertising that Nike is doing.

Performed correctly, you should know to the penny how much it costs you to generate a sale. The mission of marketing is not to create a general awareness of your brand or your product. The one and only purpose of your marketing is to sell.

If a Madison Avenue-style ad campaign is like a nuclear bomb that hits everyone in an area, a direct mail marketing campaign is more like precision surgery. That's why direct mail is still the most cost-effective advertising there is.

If you remember nothing else you've read in this entire book, I urge you to remember these nine points:

1) Write about what your reader wants, not about what you want.

2) You can succeed if you write a poor letter for the right list (that is to the right people), but the best letter in the world cannot work to the wrong list.

3) Craft headlines and sub-headlines that will grab the interest of your reader.

4) Persuade your reader with facts and reasons, not fantastic claims and empty hype.

5) Keep your reader's interest with fascinating details and narrative (like Stephen King) that make it easier to keep reading than to skip what is being said.

6) Craft an offer no intelligent reader can pass up.

7) Don't make your guarantee a boring after-thought, but instead create a super-charged guarantee that will catch your reader's attention, like Nordstrom's famous guarantee.

8) Give your reader good solid credible reasons for answering your letter today, not tomorrow.

9) Make sure your letter reads like a letter from one person to another, that it does not come across as mass advertising . . . even if economics dictate that you must mail a cheap non-personalized "Dear Friend" letter.

Whether you are writing to a few people or a million people, if you achieve these nine things, you will succeed.

If I can be of further assistance to you in your marketing efforts, send me an email at **lovesdirectmail@aol.com** or visit my Web site at:

DirectMailCopywriters.com.

I would be happy to answer any further questions you might have concerning the marketing challenges you're facing.

Sincerely,

Ben

Ben Hart
DirectMailCopywriters.com

P.S. Check out **DirectMarketingInstitute.com** for the Direct Marketing Boot Camp schedule for entrepreneurs.

The **Direct Marketing Boot Camps** takes place throughout the year. I hope to see you at the next one. I'd also very much like to get your feedback on this book. Was it helpful to you? Please send me your comments at **lovesdirectmail@aol.com.**